CONVIVIO

May you enjoy Convivio with family & friends
Lucy Luhan

CONVIVIO

Good Food.
Good Company.
Good Health.

Lucy Ann Vallera Luhan

Kua Bay Publishing LLC

First Edition

ISBN: 978-0-9981063-4-2

Dedication

My mother, Mary Concetta Vallera, an Italian immigrant, taught me and exposed our family to Italian food culture, which includes *convivio*, and the traditions of an Italian table. She worked tirelessly her entire life, preparing meals for our family and others with a passion for fresh ingredients. At the age of one hundred and five, she continued to be a loving role model and the matriarch of our family. I am forever grateful to her for instilling in me her passion for food, and family, and conviviality of the family table. I hope this book will lead others to practice and enjoy as most Italians do, the physical, psychological, social and emotional benefits of *convivio*.

I am grateful also to have had a wonderful mother-in-law, Josefa Visus Luhan, for fifty years, until she passed away at the age of one hundred and six, for having raised her son, my husband, Jorge, with food culture. Whenever work, social responsibilities, or other obligations tempted me away from the family table, my husband guided me back to *convivio*.

Biography

A first-generation Italian-American, Lucy Ann Vallera Luhan was born in Connecticut and raised in a household where traditional foods and values prevailed. She helped her extended family can fruits and vegetables grown in their own garden every summer, make their own wine every autumn, and prepare fresh pasta daily. Luhan's upbringing and passion for *convivio* led her to spend thirty-five years as a restaurateur in Southern California, and eventually inspired her to open Villa Lucia, a bed and breakfast/cooking school in Tuscany, Italy. She and her husband plan, in 2019, to spend more time in Abruzzo, Italy, the village of her ancestors. It is here where she first discovered her passion for authentic food, *convivio*, and a Mediterranean lifestyle.

Table of Contents

Foreword

by Michelle K. Luhan Nordberg, MS, RD, CDN

Imagine growing up in Southern California in the '70s and having veal parmesan and tongue sandwiches in your brown-bag school lunch. Needless to say, my lunches and our family dinners were not the customary. Lunches were more often than not leftovers stuffed into homemade bread, plus a fruit and a homemade oatmeal cookie, if we had them. That was it. Natural, genuine, real, unadulterated foods made their mark on my palette at an early age.

Sometimes these meals came with a bit of embarrassment from friends and boyfriends – I'll never forget the first time I brought my HS quarterback boyfriend over for dinner and my mother served tripe. When he asked why the chicken tasted chewier than the chicken he was used to my mother said, "Well, that's because you are eating cow stomach...." Similar exchanges happened when shark, liver or pig's feet made it onto our family-style dinner menus. As if that wasn't enough of a shock to our childhood friends, imagine their faces when they heard wine mixed with seltzer was the only available drink option (no milk) and that meals sometimes lasted over an hour, certainly over two on the weekends. The Luhan house was not where you came for TV dinners.

With time, our house and specifically our dinner table became the place where many of our friends learned about food: how to prepare it, eat it, and enjoy it. To this day I still hear stories from friends about how my family's unconventional dinner table hours gave them their first real exposure to traditional foods.

Through these meals at the table with multi-generational friends and family, and the endless hours working at my mother's Italian restaurants where she employed many of our extended family members and neighborhood friends and children, I learned to value the importance of real food, and with that the joys that come from eating and sharing with others. These experiences also influenced the career choices I later delved into, from hospitality to recipe development, dietetics, food education and wellness.

So when I started a family, it was no surprise that healthy, home-cooked meals and international foods became part of our menu rotation. And with the advent of Whole Foods and increasing health awareness at the time, serving real food was less of a challenge for me and my peer group.

And yet when my kids went off to elementary school it seemed the public-school system did not value the same healthy foods we mothers knew our children required for their growing bodies and minds. I couldn't believe the quality of food and the ingredients school children were being offered every day for lunch. And so, in 2005, together with three other moms, I started a health committee at our kids' K-12 NYC public school, Nest+m on the lower east side of Manhattan.

This preceded the efforts of New York City's Mayor Michael Bloomberg to limit trans fats and high fructose corn syrup drinks in schools. It also came before celebrity chef Jamie Oliver's valiant effort to change school food in UK and Europe.

Our movement was initially met with some resistance from the administration but when we explained our hands-on approach and presented the research on some of the harmful ingredients that were in some of the packaged foods being served, they let us make some small changes. Those little changes eventually led to new recipes for our school cafeteria and for NYC SchoolFood citywide. We initiated "Mmmm...Mondays," school food-tasting events, and educational programs that touched on sustainability, health and cultural foods. Our cafeteria staff had to work a little more to cook from scratch rather than just reheat, but they were proud of their new menus and proud to know they were making a positive change. The salad bar was more colorful and the menus more exotic and fun for the kids. We brought in olive oil, legumes, tofu, fresh and dried herbs, seaweed, pickled foods, and any other real food that we could procure from school food requisition lists. Extras were paid for by the PTA and subsidized by our committee.

It was all going well, and we were able to validate our efforts with research studies showing the health benefits of early childhood nutrition and disease prevention. We referenced articles from Walter Willett, Professor of Nutrition at the Harvard School of Public Health, Marion Nestle of NYU's Nutrition Department where I received my master's degree, The Center for Science in the Public Interest, Tufts School of Nutrition and Health and UC Berkeley's Nutrition Department. But our efforts were eventually met with the challenges many face when trying to change the system. And after four years, we had to stop.

As a mother of two teenagers, a dietitian in private practice for over 20 years and an omnivorous food enthusiast, I can't think of a more critical time to introduce families to natural real food than when their children are young. And there is no better place to do so than at home with family, at the table together. Convivial experiences, I believe, can lead to health and happiness at all stages of life. It's never too late to set the table and invite some friends over... Bon Appetit!

INTRODUCTION

*"A pleasant meal best humble or elaborate, accepted and savored, simply for
what it should be, nothing more than the stimulus for the ultimate pleasures of the table,
good passionate conversation."*

—Brillat-Savarin

My husband and I were spending the holidays in the Abruzzo region of Italy when a family of six entered the restaurant and hung their wraps on the hooks decorating the walls of the cozy trattoria, Gino's in Sulmona. Watching that family eat their meal together reminded me of the importance of *convivio*. The poet Dante Alighieri brought the term *"convivio"* into use in his writing of Il *Convivio, (The Banquet),* describing table time as being an important time to gain wisdom and knowledge along with food and good company as seen in this affresco, 1592, by Andrea Boscoli titled *Convivio di Dio.*

The waiter seated the newcomers next to us, then began reciting the specials of the day. The mother interrupted him once to inquire about the mixed antipasto special. The waiter took his time, giving her a detailed history about the dish. The cheese was a local brand, from the farm that produced it; in addition, he explained the history of the aged salami.

After the lengthy antipasto conversation, the waiter took the children's primo (first course) orders as we continued to watch and listen, mesmerized by the orders placed by the youngsters. The youngest child, who was maybe five years old, ordered the spaghetti with zucchini and *zafferano*, while his brother, perhaps a year older, asked for pasta with porcini mushrooms. The two older girls ordered spaghetti with *cinghiale* (wild boar sauce).

When the waiter asked for their choice of secondo (second course), the five-year-old requested sausage on the grill, his brother ordered grilled *rosticcini* (tiny strips of lamb), and both of the girls asked for the grilled lamb special. The parents ordered the mixed meat grill.

As my husband wondered if the kids could eat it all, I reminded him that the portions would be small. I wasn't surprised by the family's many courses, or their meal selections. In the Italian home, eating right is like learning a language, a total immersion from birth. Italian parents encourage children to try new tastes, even if children are hesitant to do so, which allows them to enjoy these new experiences outside the home.

The mother ordered the *contorno*, a vegetable side dish, and asked for the waiter's advice between the two specials, zucchini and broccoli rabe. He smiled and said, "Of course, the broccoli rabe would be best, being in season, and picked this morning in the garden of a local *contadino* (farmer)."

As the courses began arriving, the children participated in the conversation with their parents. I observed no restlessness or boredom as they sat at the table, despite the lack of coloring books and technical gadgets to entertain them.

As the family enjoyed the antipasto dish, the children discussed stories of their school days. What a perfect time for parents to gain insight into their children's lives, I thought. By not allowing TV or other distractions to interfere with this precious time, members of this family could focus on each other.

Ten minutes after finishing their antipasto, the pasta course was served. While waiting for our own secondo, I overheard the family's conversation about a soccer game. Nobody was anxious to be served, and nobody complained. When the pasta dishes were placed in front of each person, they all picked up their silverware and deftly swirled the pasta around their forks, balancing it against their dishes.

The children skillfully handled their cutlery to separate the meat from the bones of their food while their mother served equal portions of the sautéed broccoli rabe onto each plate. It was a relief not to hear the typical American youngster's question, "What is that green stuff?" possibly never having had broccoli rabe.

Watching these children consume their vegetables led me to another memory from our days of hosting guests at Villa Lucia. Many of the American families who stay at our B&B bring packaged noodles in their suitcases for their youngsters. I was horrified when one mother explained to me that she knew it was unhealthy, and that the processed item was full of salt, additives, and chemicals—but she fed this to her child because he loved them! Why did she ever give it to him?

One day while they were visiting, I prepared tomato sauce using cherry tomatoes from the garden and homemade pasta. This mother gave her son a choice between eating his packaged noodles and what I had cooked for dinner. Naturally, he chose the familiar food. Here was an opportunity for her son to have a new culinary experience, yet that mother had allowed her five-year-old to make the decision. This was the formula for dietary disaster.

When the family dining next to us cleaned their plates of their *secondo*, the waiter asked if he could bring them anything else. The parents requested their espresso and the children each responded with a *"no, grazie."* Although desserts can be the pride of a pastry chef, Italians aren't usually tempted by sugary concoctions after a satisfying meal. They would be more apt to settle for seasonal fruit and a selection from the cheese cart. Most restaurants offer a *macedonia* (fresh fruit salad) for those Italians desiring a sweet. Although I have observed changes in Italian youth as they adopt more and more of the Western culture that says, "save room for desert," which I never heard in Italy being that the desert is not the most important course.

As the family prepared to leave, I glanced at my watch and realized that over two hours had passed. For Italians, life revolves around the table whenever possible. That is certainly not true in the United States, where a family is often experiencing eating simultaneously while doing other activities, watching a movie, TV or working in the office. Another big difference is Italians have their children enjoy adult foods rather than eat from a children's menu. Grandchildren Luca and Dante eat everything even at restaurants like Ginos, here with chef Lucia and their dad.

I am not a doctor, nutritionist, or food scientist, but the fact that Italians continue to enjoy more longevity than any other people in Europe motivated me to discover why. This led me to compare Italians to Americans. The Americans have the greatest available income in the Western world yet continue to lead the world in food-related diseases and disorders. This inspired me to share my personal observations in the two countries I love.

The Greeks defined *diaitan* (diet), as "a way of life." For Italians, that includes *convivio*, time at the family table, the antithesis of fast food dining and a means to a healthier individual, family life and nation.

There is no authentic food culture in the United States. Many Americans seem to have a dysfunctional relationship with food as a result. Italians linger at the table while Americans eat and run. In Italy, there is a set time to eat meals. In the U.S., we can eat twenty-four hours a day. In general, Italians seek out high-quality meals, whereas most Americans favor availability. Italians will often invite lonely diners to their table; they believe the more the merrier.

According to the Organization for Economic Cooperation and Development, Americans have the highest amount of disposable income in the world. Italy doesn't even make the top five. Yet, the World Economic Forum reports that Americans spend less on food—just 6.4 percent of our household income—than any other industrialized nation.

In its 2017 comparison of 163 different countries for its Global Health Index, Bloomberg calculated a "health score" based on the likelihood of mortality by disease or injury, life expectancy at various ages, and probability of survival at key times. Italy, with its pasta eaters and wine drinkers, came out on top with a score of 93.11, while the U.S. ranked only 34th with a health score of 73.05. I have attempted to explain some of the reasons for this in *Convivio*.

I never imagined that the five-hundred-year-old abandoned farmhouse that I saw on a whim while visiting Tuscany, Italy, in 1985 would become my home, a cooking school, and a B&B, enriching my life. If I had given our guests keys to their rooms, along with coffee and croissants, instead of inviting them to our Italian table, we would never have had the opportunity to share stories and enjoy each other's company, thanks to *convivio*.

I am proud to be an American and grateful for all my native country has given me. But, when comparing food cultures, I feel fortunate to have had Italian immigrant parents who had me experience their culinary traditions and enriched my life with *convivio*.

1

La Panarda, The Longest Meal

"People are held together by the mystic cord of memory."

—ABRAHAM LINCOLN

When I was seven years old, I saw my grandmother's Italian kitchen for the first time, and my life was transformed. Even now, decades later, I vividly remember the shiver of delight that ran through my body when my eyes rested for the first time on her massive oak table and then moved on to take in miles of shiny copper pots and pans lining the walls—a necessary number, it turned out, since my mother's thirteen siblings, extended family members, and friends were constantly streaming through her door and always stayed for a meal.

Permeating that kitchen in Italy was a strong, unfamiliar, almost offensive odor. Wrinkling my nose in disgust, I tugged on my mother's blouse.

"What's that smell?" I whispered.

"Grandma's homemade olive oil," my mother replied.

Little did I know that, one day, I would be making my own olive oil in Italy, and dedicating my life to recreating and sharing the *convivio* I experienced at home and around my grandmother's table during that first visit to Italy in 1948.

Both of my parents grew up in a small farm town in Abruzzo, in the hills along Italy's east coast. With his amazing tenor voice, my father studied opera, hoping to one day become a professional opera singer. Unfortunately, economic times were tough in 1920, so at the age of fifteen, he decided to accompany his father on a trip to America. With limited English skills, he was unable to follow his dreams in music. Instead, he sought employment in construction, along with many of his compatriots, in Hartford, Connecticut.

On a return trip to Italy, he met a pretty young woman who sang in the church choir, and pursued her despite her father's objections. Over time, he was able to convince her father, a prominent landowner, that he would be able to provide a decent life for her across the ocean.

My parents were married in March 1932 in Pratola Peligna, their small hometown in Abruzzo. At the same time, some ten thousand miles away in Buenos Aires, Argentina, a young bride and her husband were expecting their first child, a son to be named Jorge Enrique Luhan. He would later become my husband.

Soon after their wedding, Dad and his father boarded the ocean liner *Roma* and headed back to America. My mom, pregnant with my oldest sister, Rose Aida, followed my father later. They settled into a modest apartment building surrounded by other Italian immigrants, many of them from Abruzzo. Dad used his basic cooking skills to make a living as a tavern grill entrepreneur. He enjoyed serving his *paisani*, the homestyle cooking they missed so much.

Two years later, my sister Mary Concetta was born. Mom focused on her two little girls, while Dad worked long hours at the tavern. My mother missed her big family, acres of land, and pets back in Italy. It was wartime, and she had to endure bomb sirens, blacked-out windows, and long hours indoors. When she did venture out, she often experienced prejudice due to Italy's aggression as part of the Axis powers. Her lack of English complicated matters even more. When I was born in 1940, Jorge Enrique Luhan was making his first communion.

Mr. and Mrs. Attilio Vallera
request the honor of your presence
at the Christening of their daughter
Lucy
on Sunday, June 1, 1941
at 3:30 P.M.
at Venetian Hall, 36 Market St.
Hartford, Conn.

The biggest joy in my mother's otherwise lonely life was Sunday *pranzo*. Dad worked long hours, but was always home on Sundays when Mom prepared and served this ritual feast to our family, friends, and neighbors. Everyone ate together at the oversized table in our small apartment, just as they had back in Italy. Some of the friendships built then lasted a lifetime. My mother's neighbor, Amy Spirito, and she have been friends for over eighty years. Their kids were playmates and, years later, Amy's son Joe married my sister Mary. Amy is now one hundred and six, and lives on her own in Connecticut. She travels to California to visit our family, and it's wonderful to see these two centenarians spend time together, my mother now one hundred and five and Amy one hundred and six.

Mom served espresso at the end of Sunday *pranzo*, and afterward Dad would lead everyone in a lively sing-along. They sang renditions of old Neapolitan songs, which always included popular tunes like "O Sole Mio" and made everyone nostalgic for the homeland. After the guests departed, Dad would listen to opera on his huge console radio record player. If he missed his favorite Sunday opera broadcast, he would play his favorite 78-rpm records. As children, we didn't really understand the words, but we enjoyed listening to Dad sing songs from Enrico Caruso, the legendary Neapolitan opera singer. Although Caruso died in 1921 at the young age of 48, his voice lived on in our home for years.

Dad's love of opera inspired him to name us after his favorite operas. Rose, my oldest sister, was given the middle name "Aida" because of Verdi's Ethiopian princess. Dad's love of Schubert's "Ave Maria" led my parents to name their second daughter Mary Concetta, which was also my mother's name. As for Lucia, I'm not sure if I was named after the emotionally fragile Lucia in Donizetti's opera, *Lucia di Lammerermoor,* or after one of Dad's favorite songs, "Santa Lucia."

One morning a year before my birth in 1940, my sisters tell me they saw mother crying after opening a letter from Italy. The envelope had a black border, which indicated an announcement of a death. Dad was horrified by the news that his mother had died, especially because of the sheer distance between him and his mother for many years. Still today, whenever we hear popular singers sing "Mamma," a Neapolitan song which my father often sang at Italian festivals, my sisters and I are reminded of Dad's sadness during this time. The song details the feelings of a young man missing his mother, and he promises to never leave her side again. My sisters and I sang it for my mother on her 100th birthday, promising to never leave her side.

My father worked long hours, so when he had an opportunity to sell his restaurant in 1948 he jumped at the chance. The timing coincided with my maternal grandfather falling ill in Italy, so my parents decided to visit their native Abruzzo for the first time in fifteen years. My sisters couldn't miss their high school classes, but I was lucky enough to accompany them. Here is my passport picture with my mom and with my parents on the boat.

What I remember most from that first childhood visit to Abruzzo is the food and art of dining, or what the Italians call *convivio*. The word comes from the Latin con, meaning "with," and *vivere*, meaning "to live." It is commonly used in Italy to refer to a family meal, feast, reception, or banquet, as described by Dante, seven hundred years ago.

Since it's a mountainous region, Abruzzo was cut off from the rest of the world for centuries. This is evident not only in the traditions of the region's people, but in the way they prepare dishes using authentic local products, creating a cuisine

free of influence by the outside world. Abruzzo's cuisine, one of the best in Italy, includes wine and olive oil praised for their quality and taste, along with extraordinary pastas known throughout the world. Because of the mountainous terrain, large animals were uncommon; many people worked as shepherds and creatively served lamb, pork, and goat.

As a child, I bonded with my grandmother's animals on that visit, especially my favorite goat, one that I watched being born. I drank goat's milk every day in Italy, just as my mother and her siblings had done during their childhoods.

My favorite animal of all was a donkey named Bella. My grandfather used Bella to pull a small cart, and during my visit, Grandpa used to walk beside the cart as I rode, feeling very much like an American princess being driven to meet her long-lost Italian relatives, all of whom fawned over me.

Fiercely proud of their culinary traditions, the Abruzzese are as well known for their hospitality as they are for their gastronomical creations. One of the best examples of this is their traditional *banchetto della panarda*. *La panarda* is known as "the longest meal in the world" and is a medieval tradition that demonstrates just how much value the Abruzzese place on the importance of life at the table.

The origin of this tradition is fascinating. Legend has it that during medieval times, the mother of a newborn went to fetch water from the town well. Upon her return, she was horrified to see her baby in a wolf's mouth. She could do nothing other than to pray to St. Anthony. Her prayers were answered when the wolf released the infant, and the

Garlic sagra with friends in Sulmona

young mother demonstrated her gratitude to by promising to feed others with a long feast. *La panarda* became a celebration known for its avalanche of delicious dishes, made with pride and served at a leisurely pace. Today, this tradition is still practiced in Abruzzo on special occasions.

Because Abruzo was a poor region, feasting was an act of defiance against famine, born out of the fear that hunger could return. To this day, pagan feast and religious events are celebrated as rituals of thanks to the gods while enjoying the fruits of the season. Every harvest culminates with a *sagra*, a festival of a seasonal food item, prepared to be enjoyed in various dishes with family and friends, maintaining the tradition of ancient villages. A festival never to be missed in our town is the *sagra* of the red garlic, native to

Abruzzo, known

only by gourmets seeking the best garlic in the world.

Aglio rosso di Sulmona, grown where my ancestors came from, is known for its medicinal properties such as the high concentration of allicon, an antibiotic substance, as well as its delicate flavor, intense aroma and shelf life. Most garlics are treated chemically for shelf life after they are harvested. These reddish purple jackets are usually braided after two weeks of drying out after the harvest so that air can circulate between the bulbs. Without chemicals, they last almost a year. Most kitchens in Abruzzo or in those of gourmets around the globe decorate their kitchens with a braid, as I have done in my Tuscan kitchen, or a circle, as I have in my Abruzzese kitchen. Once used, this colorful, medicinal garlic, necessary for authentic Abruzzese cuisine, has no substitute.

My treasure chest of early Italian memories began in Abruzzo and includes that special traditional ritual, la panarda. I don't remember the dishes we ate, but I can easily recall the festive feel of that day. Loud table conversations were carried on, with everyone appearing to be talking, gesturing, or arguing at once. Even the most heated arguments ended with lots of laughter and singing.

The daily meals around my grandmother's table had a similar feel. Older children were seated at one end of the table, preschool children sat between their parents in the middle, and adults occupied the other end. I sat by my mother's side, constantly tugging at her skirt, trying to get the English translations.

I don't recall any coloring books, crayons, puzzles, or games to occupy my time at the table. The youngest children sat quietly on their mothers' laps, fascinated by the noise, laughter, and passing plates.

Experiencing life together at the table from birth, Italian children learn early on to accept and embrace mealtimes as one of the highlights of the day. Back then, all businesses closed for lunch. Streets were empty, playgrounds were deserted, and telephones, if available, were ignored or even taken off the hook. Children ate whatever the adults did. Tasting these different flavors allowed them—and me— to enjoy those foods later in life. By the time I actually learned what I had been eating—snails, tripe, sweetbreads, liver, hearts, pig's feet, fish eggs, and ox tails—I had already learned to love them!

As young as I was, I realized that life at the table in Italy was similar to the *convivio* I had already experienced at my mother's table in Connecticut. Setting the table always included a dish of olives and farm fresh vegetables such as fennel, carrots, celery, and radishes to nibble on, and a small dish of olive oil speckled salt for dipping before the meal. Flowers rarely occupied the center of the table. In their place were the omnipresent bottles of homemade olive oil and wine, returned to the sideboard when not needed at the table. After dinner, the bottles changed places with a set of small glasses and bottles of digestives. There was always a basket of mixed nuts in their shells on the table for us to crack, and fresh fruits for everyone to enjoy after the meal, extending conversation and table time.

Three or four courses were common and always included a light soup or pasta dish, followed by a small portion of meat along with an avalanche of colorful fresh garden vegetables. At the time I had no idea that the delicious soups I thought were made with chicken broth were actually based on pigeon broth. Everything was simple, yet provided a feast of flavors. Homemade pasta, *maccheroni alla chitarra*, an Abruzzese specialty, was usually served with meat sauce. The meal usually ended with dessert, which consisted of Grandma's homemade cheeses and fruits from her garden.

I never could understand how the pigeons knew the hour of the midday meal. Disappearing in the morning, they would not be seen again until the church bells chimed the midday hour. As we would set the table, Grandma's pigeons would appear on the ledge of their coop. They would eat what I gave them, scraps of our Mediterranean diet, and then linger there the entire time that we rested at the table. In our hurried world, as most people seemed to neglect that important ingredient of time at the table, Grandma's Italian pigeons knew. They ate together making lots of noise as if imitating us, chirping away in a language of their own, maybe laughing, maybe singing, maybe talking about us, but one thing was for sure, they were happily enjoying *convivio*.

The Italian Girl

"Let food be thy medicine and medicine thy food."

—HIPPOCRATES

One particular experience forever carved in my memory from my Connecticut childhood was a visit to a doctor's office with my mother when I was ten years old. She had made the appointment because she wasn't feeling well, apparently exhausted from work. The doctor gave her a prescription. During my mother's follow-up visit a few months later, the doctor was so impressed with her results that he told her there was no need to continue the medication.

"Ma che pillola?" (What pill?) she asked, and explained that she had decided to eat more fresh greens from the garden instead of taking the pills. That day influenced how I would nourish my own family years later, following her example and making an effort to let food be our medicine whenever possible.

The cuisine of my childhood is known today as the Mediterranean Diet, but it had no name in those years. Organic farming hadn't gained popularity yet in the U.S., but in Italy, it was a way of life. Accustomed to fresh, local foods, immigrants sought this same quality in their adopted homeland.

For my parents, this meant using vegetables and fruits from their own garden, or from a neighbor or friend. They only bought meat from a reliable source: a friend's farm, a recognized breeder, or a butcher with a good reputation. Meat had to be ground in their presence, and my parents always approved of the meat selection before it entered the grinding machine. Sometimes my mother purchased the meat and ground it at home. When they bought chickens, the birds were purchased at a local hatchery. My parents knew how the birds had been raised and what they were fed.

As Catholics, we never ate meat on Fridays, only fish. If fresh fish wasn't available, my parents might settle for one of the few canned items in their pantry, either sardines or anchovies. Or, if inclement weather or distances prohibited fresh purchases, they relied on smelly, salty, hard-as-rock *baccalà*.

Baccalà is fresh cod that has been beheaded, split, salted, and hung to dry. It was inexpensive, could be stored for months, and, after a good desalting soak, could be served in various dishes. As a child, I hated the smell of the kitchen whenever Dad brought home the thick white baccalà, but knowing that after a three-day cold water soak it would become one of my favorite dishes made it easier to tolerate.

Our practice of eating only fresh produce meant that we ate what was seasonally available. Again, my parents were ahead of their time in this regard. Every season brought exciting changes to our diet, and its pleasures. When the sun-ripened tomato season began, for instance, Mom would incorporate tomatoes into every meal, from appetizer to main course, knowing the season would be short-lived. The garden's first crop of fava beans in early spring inspired us to excitedly guess what the first dish of the season might be: fava bruschetta, fava pasta sauce, fava vegetable dish, or fava *frittata*? Or Dad might simply put bunches of fresh fava beans on the center of the dinner table after we'd eaten, and we would all sit around shelling them and eating them raw as a dessert.

My parents worked hard for twelve years before they were able to purchase a home in a nice neighborhood. Our house had a large backyard for Grandpa to convert into his vegetable garden, a must for every Italian family, and a kitchen attached to the dining room so that we could all talk while we cooked and ate meals together.

It wasn't long in that new neighborhood before I became known, embarrassingly, as "the Italian Girl," and rumors soon spread around the elementary school that I knew how to cook. My reputation led me to be asked to do a demonstration in cooking class, which attracted the attention of our local paper, *The Hartford Times*. Talk about foreshadowing! At the same time thousands of miles away in Argentina, Jorge was training for the Argentinian Olympic rowing team.

Our middle-class neighborhood in Hartford was populated mostly with Jewish families. When summer vacation came, the neighborhood kids would vanish off to camp, while I passed each day around a bath-sized tub of boiling water packed with ripe tomatoes from our garden. With burning fingers, I helped my sisters, aunts, cousins, and mother peel bushelsful of our garden tomatoes. We would fill hundreds of canning jars to supply us until the next tomato season. As a kid, I couldn't understand why we didn't just buy cans of tomatoes at the market like other people did. Whenever I dared ask this question, Mom always gave the same answer: "What you don't see, you don't put in your stomach. What kind of tomatoes do they put into the cans? Nobody can see the quality."

After tomato season, we canned our fresh peaches, pears, and vegetables, and Mom made her fantastic *giardinera* (vegetables in vinaigrette). Even the unripe green tomatoes, the last of the season left on the vines, were pickled and added to the *giardinera*. Mom's *giardinera* complemented our delicious cold weather dish of *bollito misto*, vegetables and meats cooked in a hearty broth.

Knowing my family was different from many of our neighbors left me feeling envious and even inferior. Halfway through summer, most of our neighborhood friends returned, only to leave again for another camp or vacation. "Oh, to be Jewish!" I would think, as I helped my family pick figs to dry or make into sweet jam.

My children and grandchildren may never understand my attachment to Grandpa's grape press at the entrance of our home in Tuscany. My mother wondered why it was the only thing I requested of her possessions when moving from Connecticut in the 1960s. The press traveled with me from our home in Connecticut to two different locations in California, then back to Italy when we moved  overseas. Visitors coming to our front door see it as another old artifact without understanding its significance, but seeing the old wooden level reminds me to be proud of my Italian culture, and grateful to my parents for all of their hard work. When I was a child, I knew summer was turning into fall when a truckload of muscatel grapes arrived, signaling the time to begin the process of making our homemade wine.

Thus, began another extended family project. I knew little about the process back then, other than the fun we had watching the men pouring crates of grapes into the top receptacle of Grandpa's grape press. Dad and my uncles then turned the wooden handle that lowered a thick, flat wooden disk attached to a vertical pole at the center, squeezing the juice out of the grapes into a bucket below the press. Afterward, they carefully poured the juice into oak barrels, where it would undergo the fermentation process. This eventually led to the house wine sitting on our table every night.

Mom continued to make wine even after dad died, until my husband convinced her that a popular inexpensive commercially-sold burgundy was just as good as her labor-intense homemade wine. Following his advice winemaking ended in our family, at least until we moved to Italy, twenty-five years later. Before my father's old grape press arrived in Italy, Jorge decided to make his own upon seeing an old cement pressing cubicle in our basement. He managed to make an excellent Chianti for three years and then decided to join me in my effort to make good olive oil; we removed our grape vines to plant more olive trees and the cement stamping structures to make room for our olive

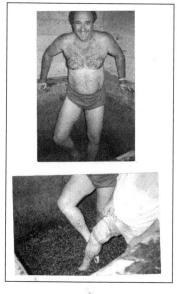

oil storage. Newport Beach's once famous plastic surgeon is seen here pressing grapes on their way to becoming our homemade Chianti table wine.

In the United States, additional sulfites are often added to imported wines sold to the public. Headaches are a common complaint among wine drinkers, especially ones who overindulge. Added sulfites have been identified as a possible cause. We never added chemicals or sulfites to our homemade wine, and I don't recall my relatives ever complaining of morning headaches after drinking it, which may be due to other factors.

As children, we were always given a little wine to color our drinking water at dinner. We were taught to respect the beverage, appreciate its taste, and enjoy it as a complement to many delicious dishes. It certainly was better than learning from our peers or others outside of the home.

As the grape pulp fermented in the barrels on its way to becoming fine ruby wine, we wasted no time moving on to the next group project: making our own sausage. The men cut pounds of pork shoulder into small chunks, ready to meet the blades of our sausage machine, a must in every immigrant's household. Dad would say, "Never buy anything stuffed, since you don't know with what."

My mom and aunts would spice up a cup or more of pork, fry it, and taste it to check for seasoning. We loved tasting the spiced pork in the frying pan. If the flavor met with my mother's approval, the spiced pork would start its journey into the machine's funnel circled with animal intestines that she had cleaned and salted days before.

Being the youngest, it was my job to needle every few inches as the spiced meat wiggled its way out of the funnel into the intestine casing. This allowed air to escape, so that the raw meat could dry in our cold cellar. My mom and aunts tied the sausage into links, forming rows and rows of fifty-plus links, which decorated the ceiling of our cellar as they hung to dry for our winter meals.

After school, my friends would come by, and I would often take them down to the cellar to break off links from the hanging rows to eat. Never did I take into consideration, as we enjoyed the aged sausage, the hard labor that had gone into making it. My Jewish friends and neighbors were as jealous of my cellar as I was of their summer life. I always wondered if it was living through the Depression that led my parents to become self-sufficient, creating their private extensive supermarket in our cellar. It was in my teens that I learned it was because of distrust for American food in those days. My parents always reminded us how fortunate we were to have been born and raised and to live in the most industrial country in the world and would repeat, "Learn English, work hard and follow your dreams." But dad always added, "Eat Italian."

With our canning done, wine made, and sausage hung decoratively in our cellar, we were ready for winter. When cold weather appeared, it signaled the time for polenta, a thick cornmeal mush eaten throughout Europe in various forms. Today's commercially-sold fine grain and instant polenta cornmeal was unfamiliar to my mother. She used only the freshly stone-ground cornmeal that she received from her sister in Italy, or from an Italian immigrant who had a source for the rustic, unrefined stone-ground cornmeal.

My mother made polenta in the unique way of her Abruzzo upbringing. My sisters and I always got excited when we saw Mom take out the long polenta board, which was only a little smaller than our kitchen table. On polenta days, there was no table to set since we would be eating off the board; the more people who joined us, the more fun it was.

Like so many of our traditional meals, making polenta in our house was a family project, with everyone taking part. My mother started the process by slowly adding handfuls of the cornmeal to a pot full of hot simmering water, letting it slide gently between the fingers of her left hand. If added in haste or into boiling water, the result would be a solid mass.

With her right hand, Mom would stir the polenta in only one direction to avoid creating lumps. After a few minutes, she allowed my sisters and me to take turns stirring the coarse stone-ground cornmeal into the enormous copper polenta pot of hot water. We used a long-handled wooden paddle to avoid being burned by splattering polenta. Mom supervised the thirty-five to forty-five minutes of constant stirring. When the polenta peeled away from the pot, it was finally ready.

Dad then poured the hot polenta all over the board and we helped spread it out to the edges. Mom ladled hot, freshly made tomato sauce over the polenta. She also topped the polenta with a variety of meats, including our homemade sausage. Then the real fun began as we devoured every last piece bit off the board, giggling at each other's tomato-sauce-painted faces. As we all forked our way through the polenta, we often made designs,

connecting them to each other. Sometimes the design would be the world map, with my sisters and me using forks to draw the United States and Europe. The design always included the boot of Italy. The more we ate, the more of the world was revealed.

Years later, when questioning my adult children on their most precious memories, they always referred to our time around the dinner table with family, friends, and visitors who always seemed to pop in unexpectedly. When asked their favorite days, the answer was unanimous: polenta days. I feel fortunate that my parents, as Italian-Italians, maintained their tradition. I, as a first-generation Italian-American, tried my best to continue to do so. Unfortunately, as much as they all loved polenta days in their youth, my children, American-Italians, rarely find time to take part in this tradition. Their children, American-Americans, are adopting the mores and mannerisms of their country, and I am sad to say they will likely allow another old-world tradition to vanish.

In retrospect, my family's food traditions were often tedious and labor-intensive, yet these traditions also comprise some of my most cherished memories. We all looked forward to making food and meals together because we could have fun sharing stories, laughter, and current events as we worked. Yes, there were chores involved in making homemade meals, but it never felt like drudgery. The joy of the family at the table, the *convivio*, made it all worthwhile.

As a group, Italian immigrants like my parents typically insulated themselves from the rest of American society by keeping company with their own extended families and maintaining their traditions. They were often criticized and faced prejudice. What kept them going was their commitment to their extended family and their *paesani*, friends from the same place of origin. Most were willing to work long hours and accept low wages to compete with other immigrant groups, particularly the Irish, who had the advantage of speaking the language. Working hard all week meant that on weekends they loved to revel in the simple pleasures of dance, music, food, and friends, sharing life and *convivio* at the table as they had in Italy.

I adored my family and loved many of our Italian traditions, but there is no question that I was also embarrassed by them from time to time—especially when it came to knowing how different our food culture was from everyone else's.

Take breakfast, for instance. While my peers were gobbling down cereal before school, our breakfast usually consisted of eggs prepared a variety of ways, unless my mother made hot oatmeal. On special days, the aroma of Mom's homemade cinnamon rolls would be our wake-up call. If she was too hurried to make anything, Mom simply beat two eggs for each of us with a shot of Marsala wine and a little sugar, never considering salmonella.

Years later, while making the dessert *zambaglione* in my restaurant, I realized that what Mom was essentially giving us for nourishment was a shot of wine with our breakfast eggs. When I asked her about this a few years ago, she assured me it was just a drop, adding, "It didn't do you any harm, did it?"

As a child, I didn't understand why we couldn't just eat cold cereal like my friends. My mother argued against it, saying she couldn't understand how cereal could sit on the grocery store shelf for months. "Something has to preserve it," she said. Years later, of course, I learned that Mom was right: those so-called "enriched" cereals contained hidden additives.

I also tried to convince Mom that there was nothing wrong with the new, frozen, "just add water" orange juice so popular then. "Just eat the orange," she answered, pointing to the large bowl of fruit that was a permanent fixture on our dining room table. "Do you know what is in that can? If you want juice, just squeeze!" She wouldn't even let me get away with squeezing it the night before, demanding, "Why not do it in the morning?"

Lunches certainly didn't make me feel any more American. My Italian lunch bag was such an embarrassment for me in grammar school that I used to hide my sandwiches. Other kids had peanut butter and jelly spread on store-bought, spongy white bread. Why did I have to be so different?

My mother's freshly-baked, rustic bread had a chewy crust and earthy flavor; it was delicious eaten alone or with a fine meal. This tasty item was never absent from the table. In fact, my parents had a saying: *"Senza il pane, tutto diventa orfano."* ("Without good bread, all the rest becomes an orphan.")

For most Italian immigrants, commercially-prepared white breads weren't even worthy of the title of "bread," so I had sandwiches on Mom's thick slices. She filled the sandwiches with prosciutto, salami, homemade sausages, all kinds of cheeses, or even dinner leftovers: roast beef, tongue, pork, sweetbreads, or brain croquettes. On Fridays, since we couldn't eat meat, my sandwiches consisted of grilled eggplant, zucchini, tuna fish, *frittata*, cheese, or greens like the Swiss chard from Grandpa's garden. Our lunch always included fresh fruit, too. Only on very special days did we have a treat: Mom's homemade oatmeal cookies with raisins.

While eating, I would try to hide the inside of the sandwich so that I wouldn't have to see my classmates frown with disgust as they asked, "What is that?" It was only in high school that my sandwiches started to become popular and I had a chance to taste my very first peanut butter sandwich on a trade. I found it to be strange, yet I traded for peanut butter sandwiches occasionally anyway, giving up homemade sausage sandwiches covered with roasted peppers for something that came out of a jar and was smeared on a tasteless white sponge. I realized after a few trades that the soggy bread smeared with pureed peanuts with hydrogenated fats, salt, and sugar tended to leave me hungry.

Dinners for us were also different from the dinners I ate at friends' houses. Our evening meals always included vegetables from the garden or from our family basement, our "personal supermarket." Beans, left to dry for the winter months, made frequent appearances at dinner, always a different variety and preparation.

During my mother's time, beans were considered the "meat of the poor" because they provided an inexpensive source of protein to so many people during years of hardship. Today, beans are slowly being recognized in America as a truly valuable and delicious food option. In fact, my B&B cooking class attendees continue to request my "famous" bean recipe. It's so simple that I can hardly call it a recipe. All I do is sauté lots of fresh, thinly-sliced leeks in good quality olive oil. When the leeks are soft, I add big meaty Spanish beans, also called corona or butter beans. I use dried beans, soaked overnight, but most of our attendees use canned beans, which are fine. I let this simmer for a while, allowing the bean juice and leeks to make a succulent dish. Little else is needed to finish the dish, but I like a little hot red pepper and salt to finish it off.

This simple "recipe" has brought customers to our B& B and has even taught non-bean eaters to appreciate the taste of a simple bean. When the recipe was published in a newspaper, the title was "Lucy's beans." I wish I could have been written up for something more complicated!

When dinners in my parents' Connecticut home included meat, this was usually a roast on Sunday, thinly sliced, dressed with natural juices, and complemented with vegetables that would cook along with it in the pan. Mom was always frugal; when making our roast, she would bake her bread and cook all of the vegetables in the oven at the same time to save fuel. She didn't use flour to thicken gravy, soups, or sauces. She might chop a carrot or celery if a sauce needed sweetening, or puree it if it needed thickening.

Just as we'd had in Abruzzo with my grandparents, Mom always placed nibbles of fresh fennel, carrots, and celery in the center of the table, along with a little dish of Zia Michelina's homemade olive oil sent from Italy. Waiting for dinner, we would dip the vegetables into the olive oil while talking to Mom about the day's events. Before the main meal, Mom usually served a light soup, and on Thursdays and Sundays she served a homemade pasta dish.

Making fresh pasta was time consuming, but for some reason never appeared to be work. I loved watching Mom use an enormous rolling pin to stretch the dough into a thin circle measuring more than a yard in diameter. Mom would then roll two sides to the center, creating a double roll, which she deftly cut with her big knife, creating thin strips of *tagliatelli*. As kids, we helped put the pasta on mop poles balanced between two chairs to allow the pasta to dry.

"Diet" and "calories" were unfamiliar words to my mother. She never mentioned them, and there was no bathroom scale for daily weighing. Nobody skipped meals and no family member was ever absent from the table. Once, when my then husband-to-be asked my father for special permission to allow me to be absent from the evening meal when I was twenty-five years old, Dad answered, "Why can't you join us for dinner?"

Holidays meals were memorable during my childhood. As with most Italian families, everyone worked together and contributed. Dad had the big yard, Uncle Tony, the pizza oven, Uncle Eduardo, the homemade brew of *grappa*, Grandpa, his homemade wine, cousins, baskets of fresh fruits from their gardens, aunts, their specialties of homemade pastries, and mother, her homemade pasta. My parents relied on fresh, hand-selected ingredients for every meal, and that was especially true during holidays. Christmas Eve dinner traditionally consisted of seven kinds of fish, one of which was eel. One unforgettable Christmas, my mother killed and cleaned the eel, then packaged the inedible remains in newspaper and handed them to me to dump in the outside trash. Just as I was about to close the lid on the trash can, I was shocked to see the newspaper wiggle, as if its contents were attempting to escape. I ran into the kitchen to tell my mother. She was not at all surprised and explained that the fish was dead, but the movement was actually the quivering of the heart, no longer pumping with blood.

For Thanksgiving, Dad would bring us a live turkey weeks before Thanksgiving because he wanted to ensure the bird was healthy, well fed, and fattened with good food before it took the place of honor on our holiday table.

After we'd eaten our holiday meal, the women cleared the table, shook the tablecloth free of crumbs, and did the dishes in record time so they could play their game of *tombola* (bingo) in the kitchen and gossip. A large platter of fresh fruit and a bowl of mixed fresh nuts in their shells returned to their rightful places at the center of the kitchen table, where earlier there had been Dad's homemade table wine and olive oil.

One of the women would start making espresso to signify that the evening was drawing to a close. Homemade cookies might join the fruit and nuts as the aroma of freshly roasted coffee beans wafted from the espresso pot. Coffee cups were placed in the center of the dining room table for the men, along with bottles of liquors, such as anisette, *grappa*, and *sambuca*: "digestives."

When I returned to the States to attend my fiftieth-class reunion, I was surprised how everyone remembered me as "the Italian Girl" with the great cellar and garden. Some remembered walking home with me after school and stopping in our garden to enjoy the grapes from the vines on the pergola over our long garden table. Others recalled picking great white peaches from an old tree in our garden, and mourning that tree when it was struck down by lightning. Others remembered the wheel of *parmigiana* cheese they enjoyed, cutting off chunks of it with the *parmigiana* knife always found resting in its place on top of a chunk of cheese.

As I was leaving the reunion, a classmate I didn't recognize at first called me by name and commented on how he had never forgotten how sad he was when I left for Italy one summer. When I asked why, he explained that, in my absence, he couldn't go over to the house and slice the prosciutto resting on our slicing machine in our kitchen, or break off links of sausage hanging in the cellar. Most of all, he added, he had missed stopping by to see our family dining *al fresco* at that long table in the yard, which always led to an invitation to join us at the table. I then recalled very well the man before me: He was the Jewish kid whose faith my mother had questioned some sixty years ago, seeing that he loved and devoured our sausage and prosciutto. At the time, he had told my mother that since he didn't know it was pork, he thought it would be okay to eat it.

I often wonder if my classmates would have remembered me if it were not for my mom's kitchen, Grandpa's garden, and my father's cellar. I suppose being "the Italian Girl" had its advantages after all.

3

Eating Like An American

*"Always choose the finest ingredients. This will help you make a good impression.
This is the first commandment of those who are passionate about food.
It is the condition* sine qua non *for the success of a dish."*

—ARTUSI

It was uncommon for Italian parents in the 1960s to allow their daughters to leave home for college. For my parents, the expense also made it prohibitive. I accepted with dismay the fact that I would have to go to school locally. Then my sister Rose gave me the opportunity of a lifetime. Her husband, first violinist with the Minneapolis Symphony Orchestra, was often required to travel for months on tour; Rose suggested that I live with her and keep her company while he was traveling. Soon I was enrolled at Macalester College, after which I transferred to the University of Minnesota.

Rose took great care of me, and she cooked as well as my mother. However, juggling my busy school schedule with working every day after school left me only weekends to eat with her family. I took three different buses to school every morning, often in sub-zero temperatures, and would carry my breakfast with me for the long commute. For the first time, I experienced what it was like to be a true American, eating on the go and often alone, choosing foods based on ease and availability over quality.

During my college years, for example, I tried my first American salad topped with a strange, sweet, thick dressing instead of the good olive oil and vinegar my mother used. At home, the only beverages on our dinner table were water and homemade wine. Now I had a choice of milk and sodas, including Dr. Pepper—a drink that I erroneously concluded must be healthier than other sodas, given its name.

Lunch at the university cafeteria introduced me to a new world of foods in addition to those salads. Everything I ate seemed to be covered with heavy sauces, except for bratwursts, a treat that I'd never had before. They became my favorite, even though I wasn't exactly sure what was inside them.

Monday nights, I had a required weekly dinner with my sorority sisters. The girls all looked forward to these meals and I tried to fit in by showing enthusiasm. Sometimes it was an effort, like the first time I tasted a small lamb chop covered with some sweet, green, wiggly mint sauce. Another Monday, I noted that the posted menu was pork chops, my favorite meat, and I looked forward to it. But, when the dish was served, I wondered, "Where's the pork?" On my plate lay a tiny, unidentifiable piece of meat that had been floured, breaded, re-floured, breaded again, deep fried, and highly seasoned. It was accompanied by a mound of sweet, brownish-looking sauce that was supposedly made from apples, but I certainly couldn't taste them.

Staying over at my sorority house was fun. All of the girls had rooms cluttered with books, papers, and clothing. There was one strange thing, though. There were snacks everywhere, and the trash baskets were overflowing with empty soda cans, chip bags, and candy wrappers. I realized that American college students really did snack all day long. Unfortunately, it didn't take long for me to adopt this American habit.

When I transferred to the university in my sophomore year, some classes took place in an auditorium that seated hundreds. I found myself in a different seat each time, but, wherever I sat, I could see students eating in class. Hearing and smelling the food had me salivating, since I'd consumed breakfast on the bus hours earlier. After class, I would head straight to the vending machine down the hall, where I usually made poor food choices.

I also picked up another American habit during this time: doing things simultaneously. My parents considered eating at the table a daily necessity and pleasure; they often criticized Americans who ate while driving, watching TV, or sitting in a movie theater. Now I had become one of them. With my insane schedule, leisurely dining seemed like a waste of time, and I often found myself eating alone while commuting or studying.

Because I enjoyed the convenience of sandwiches from the school snack shop, I did learn to eat the soggy bread for a while, usually covered with some kind of mayonnaise mixture that hid the bad quality of the cold cuts. Scarfing the food down while completing homework assignments, I wasn't even cognizant of what I was eating. One day, however, I paused to analyze my so-called "cheese" sandwich, and realized the cheese was "processed cheese food" that couldn't compare to the cheeses I'd been raised eating: aged *parmigiana*, *provolone*, and *artigiano*-made *pecorino*. Another time, I dissected a sandwich and saw a piece of fatty meat, topped with processed cheese food and smothered with some white sweet sauce. From then on, I decided to bring sandwiches from home instead.

I lived in my warm-ups and winter clothes, so I didn't notice the weight I had put on. The day I could no longer zip up my trousers, I decided to weigh myself. Imagine my surprise when I saw that my five-foot-four body, which had weighed 105 pounds when I had arrived in Minnesota a year before, showed a gain of twenty pounds! How was that possible, when I had been skipping meals and often went to bed hungry?

When I mentioned my weight gain to some of my classmates, I discovered that many of them were also battling extra pounds. Most were on fad diets. After dieting, they would treat themselves to high-calorie snacks and meals, destroying any progress they might have made. I also began a roller-coaster ride of bad eating habits.

When Christmas holidays came, it was a great opportunity for me to learn to ski and join my classmates on winter break, but I couldn't miss a family holiday. As my classmates prepared their ski equipment for their great holiday, I got my Greyhound ticket to take me back home to Connecticut.

Christmas, like all of our holidays, was anchored by family food traditions. Shortly thereafter, I was honored at the *Pavana* debutante ball, where two of my sorority sisters flew in to surprise me and the sorority house sent me my very first dozen long-stemmed red roses.

Little did I know that in July of 1960, as I was coming out in society, my future husband Jorge was saying goodbye to his medical school colleagues and boarding a plane for America, where he would begin his internship at Salem Hospital in Massachusetts.

I had always wanted to travel, but lacked the necessary funds to do so. I saw an opportunity to travel when I applied for a scholarship program to study in Italy junior year. My subject was the Catholic Communist Crisis. At that time, Italy had the largest Communist party outside of the Iron Curtain; some feared the country would soon become a Communist state. The research I proposed involved visiting Communist villages from the north to the south of Italy. My father initially didn't approve of his twenty-year-old daughter traveling alone in a foreign country. But, thanks to my cousin Rocky, who offered to be available to travel with me to certain locations, as well as the persistent persuasion by my sisters, my father finally gave his permission for me to go.

Rocky was the brother I'd never had. He had immigrated to America as a sixteen-year-old, when I was twelve, and lived downstairs in our big home in Connecticut. I often found him holding back tears as he expressed his longing for Italy.

"We have everything here," I would tell him, but he would only say how much he missed his espresso at the neighborhood coffee bar. I offered to make him coffee, but he would shake his head.

In Italy, the coffee bar is the community gathering spot where people of all ages meet to talk, argue, laugh, play cards, play bingo, discuss the news, watch soccer games, and share neighborhood gossip. It wasn't until my study abroad trip to Italy during college that I fully understood what Rocky meant; after that, I longed for the neighborhood coffee bars in Italy as well.

Thanks to Rocky, I managed to make a U-turn back to Italian food and life at the table. We dined together during our travels, and before long, we would be joined by waiters, customers, cooks, and owners. Sometimes ten people pulled up chairs to join us. It is customary in Italy to join others or invite others to your table. Everyone we met was willing to give advice, directions, and contact information of people for me to interview, which proved to be helpful for my research.

By experiencing these Italian dinners, I quickly relearned to enjoy time at the table, eat slowly, and have small portions. Each new course would take time to arrive from the kitchen. Our meat dishes, which usually followed a pasta course, were always simply roasted, grilled, or baked to perfection. Rocky always used the olive oil bottle on the table to dribble a few drops on his meat. I learned to do this as well, enjoying the meat juices blending with the good oil to make a succulent soak for the country bread. Fifty years later, I continue to drip the liquid gold on my meat.

Rocky and I never asked for a dessert menu. All of our meals ended with whole seasonal fruits in a big bowl of ice-cold water, served with paring knives. The fruit finished off the meal perfectly. No need for the sweet dessert I'd grown accustomed to having at the end of every meal at the University.

On my way to attend the scholars' program reunion, my luggage was stolen in Sicily. I bought a change of clothes, reconstructed some of my notes, and finished the summer traveling with a plastic grocery bag in place of my suitcase. That experience in 1961 taught me how to travel with only a small carry-on suitcase, saving me hours of packing and unpacking over the years.

At the reunion, my professor heard what had happened and suggested that I go alone somewhere and try to reconstruct what I had previously written before returning to the States. I chose San Marino, the small republic independent of Italy, a safe place for a twenty-year-old female traveling alone. In my little hotel room overlooking a *piazza*, I worked day and night. Every evening I was distracted by the music, singing, and dancing of tourists and Italians enjoying *al fresco* dining below my window until the church bells chimed at midnight. I saw guests being seated at eight o'clock and noted the same guests were there when the church bells chimed midnight. I found it difficult not to join them, but stayed within my budget and continued my studies, eating a sandwich made with bread taken from the lunch basket earlier that day.

My love for Italy fueled my desire to find employment and return after graduation. My parents supported my decision under one condition: that I spend the summer after senior year living at home in Connecticut and working. I found temporary employment as assistant to the director of a hospital social services department. Toward the end of summer, I was asked to meet with a surgical resident in the hospital cafeteria to discuss a patient, and my entire future shifted direction.

The following weekend, home alone, I decided to do some baking. With my hair in pigtails, wearing my old University of Minnesota sweatshirt and singing along with Elvis's "Hound Dog," I made oatmeal cookies and homemade bread. Minutes after removing trays of cookies and *grissini* (breadsticks) from the oven, the doorbell interrupted my singing.

Hands full of dough, sweatshirt and pants decorated with flour, I found myself greeting Jorge Luhan, the handsome Argentine doctor I had met earlier that week in the cafeteria. I gaped in shock, embarrassed to think he might have heard me singing, and mortified that he was seeing me in these sloppy clothes with flour everywhere.

Jorge looked me over with a big smile. "Who are you cooking for?" he asked.

"How did you know where I live?" I asked instead of answering.

Later, Jorge would tell me that this was the day he knew I would be a part of his life forever. If I had deliberately set out to capture his heart, I couldn't have planned it better. Who could resist the aromas of cookies and fresh bread permeating the house?

That surprise visit, and a few more coffee meetings with Jorge, led me to rethink my move to Italy. I continued working at New Britain General Hospital in Connecticut for another year before going to graduate school in Boston. With little free time, I seldom saw Jorge outside of the cafeteria or in our house, where he spent his one night off each week at our table, reveling in Mom's four-course meals.

Jorge proposed after that year I spent in Boston. His marriage proposal came with three unusual stipulations. First, I was to never bring home takeout food prepared by someone unknown or packed in a Styrofoam container. It was fine if I didn't have time to cook, he said, as long as I could fry an egg.

Second, Jorge hoped that we would eat together every night at the table. I reassured him that this wouldn't be a problem for me, since this was the rule in my own family as well.

Third, if we had children, Jorge wanted me to be home when they returned from school. He explained it was important for a parent to be there if they had something to discuss that might not be able to wait.

And so I found myself in love with a man who wanted to steer my life back to the cultural traditions that I treasured so much from childhood. We were wed the following year, and I happily began our Italian-American/Argentinian table, after our honeymoon in Argentina.

4

Convivio at my Italian-American-Argentinian Table

"Food is not only taste, but also atmosphere. Food is about family and friends."

—ARTUSI

Living on the salary of a medical resident required a stringent food budget. This didn't pose a challenge for Jorge and me, however. Although we were born thousands of miles apart, my husband and I were raised with similar cuisines highlighted by eating nutritiously and economically at the table.

We did have one major culinary difference, however: popcorn. Eating popcorn was the one food habit left over from my college days. My friends had introduced me to popcorn, which we ate at any time of day or night, but especially at the movie theater. We consumed movie popcorn down to the last unpopped kernels at the very bottom of the jumbo bucket.

On my first movie date with Jorge, the aroma of fresh popcorn caused me to salivate the minute we entered the theater. I waited eagerly for him to suggest a bucket. To my surprise, we went straight to our seats. While waiting for the movie to begin, he looked over at me and whispered, "Oh, how disgusting! Look at those big buckets. How can they eat while watching a movie? Is that their dinner?"

Eager to impress him, I miserably agreed, too embarrassed to admit that I would have loved a bucket. After marriage, though, my addiction to popcorn exposed itself and, unable to change my American habit, my new husband found it easier to adopt mine. Now movie time meant popcorn time for both of us, but we smuggled our own homemade, lightly salted popcorn into the theater.

By the time our first child, Michelle, was born in 1968, we were living in a studio apartment in New York City, where Jorge had received a residency in plastic surgery at New York University Medical Center. Feeding our daughter solid foods on our budget was easy: I made her baby food out of whatever we were eating, pureeing it myself. In this way, Michelle grew accustomed to a variety of tastes from infancy and was never shy about trying new foods later on.

Michelle's first solid food was mashed bananas, which were great while traveling through Europe by car. Bananas were followed by mashed sardines, an economical source of protein. For less than twenty-nine cents a can, I could buy four jumbo headless Portuguese sardines in either a tomato or mustard base.

In spite of our budget and small apartment, Jorge would invite any foreign medical doctor visiting the hospital to our house for dinner. He sensed how lonely they might be without family and friends. Besides, to most foreigners, the unfamiliar hospital food wasn't very appetizing. Jorge's desire to welcome them to our table rewarded us with many wonderful friends. Soon our apartment at Thirty-fourth and First became a home-away-from home to many, and a place where we could enjoy *convivio*.

One night, we hosted a prominent professor of plastic surgery from Czechoslovakia, visiting on a special visa. I apparently must have apologized several times during that dinner for our small quarters and the simple meal of lasagna, salad, and fresh fruit. As the professor prepared to leave, he gave me a long hug, took a last look around our small living quarters with tears in his eyes, and asked me never to apologize for such a wonderful evening in such a beautiful setting. He said we were rich with hope and opportunity, while he had none. He didn't want to return to Communist Czechoslovakia, but had no choice. If he did not return, his family would be jailed or executed. As we said goodbye, I realized he was right. Jorge and I really were rich, because we had unlimited freedom and hope.

Following Jorge's residency in New York, he accepted a fellowship at Queen Victoria Hospital in England. It was an exciting opportunity because this renowned hospital pioneered plastic surgery treatments for severe burn victims, including members of the Royal Air Force injured during World War II.

On our way to England, we decided to visit my family in Italy and then travel through France and Spain. At the time, our finances were so constrained that we thought we might never have the opportunity to see those countries again. Our first European stop was in Abruzzo, Italy, to introduce my husband to my Italian relatives. What was supposed to be only a day's visit became two weeks of total relaxation. During our stay, my relatives introduced Jorge to his first *panarda*. Like an enjoyable play of many acts, time passed unnoticed.

Pacentro

Since my grandparents had passed away, the meal was prepared by my extended family, who took great pleasure in working together to create dishes. They amazed me with their ability to take simple farm products and turn them into a glorious feast, using family recipes passed down through generations.

We had dinner one night with my cousin, Marquis Emmanuele Transmonti, whose family was the last nobility to occupy the Palace in Introdacqua. They lived in the nearby town of Pacentro, a beautiful, quaint medieval village in central Italy, in the Apennines mountain range.

The conversation was fascinating. Because of its geographical location tucked in the mountain pass, Pacentro was one of the few villages spared during WWII aerial bombardments. Unfortunately, when the Italians surrendered in September 1943, the Nazis occupied the town. They raided the feudal domains of many powerful families, including my cousin's. Their crops were destroyed, animals slaughtered, and belongings stolen. At my cousin's villa, bullet holes were still evident on frescos where the soldiers had practiced shooting.

By the time my cousin had reached the conclusion of his story, talking about how the British troops had liberated the town in June of 1944, Jorge and I realized we had been sitting at the table for four hours. When we commented on how much we had eaten while lost in conversation, my cousin attempted to convince my husband that food digests more easily with laughter. He also demonstrated to Jorge that a few bounces in the chair after each course also assisted digestion.

Everything was homemade and locally sourced. The vegetables were grown on the farm and the trout came from the lake on my aunt's property. The rabbit meat was from the animals she fed every day, and her antipasto of prosciutto, salami, sausages, and cheeses was made from the family's well-fed animals.

The idea of so many dishes might seem gluttonous to anyone hearing the list of what was put on the table, but the portions were small and there were no heavy caloric sauces to drown the fresh ingredients. Our meals may very well have had fewer calories than a fast-food meal today.

We regretted having to leave Abruzzo, but after extending our stay for ten wonderful days, we headed to Paris. When we reached the city, I was nursing Michelle in the front seat of our rented Renault when Jorge asked me to check the map and find a place to stay. He then added, "hang on," and circled the Arc de Triomphe for the fourth time.

Trying to read the map, nurse three-month-old Michelle, and figure out where we were, made me nauseous. It took all of my willpower not to vomit. Fortunately, I caught sight of the sign for the Gardens of Luxembourg, which I recalled earlier as a green area on the map, and directed Jorge toward it. He took another lap around the traffic circle and followed my directions. That quick decision led to a lifelong friendship that enriched our lives forever after.

Outside of the gardens, on the corner of Rue de Fleurs and Rue de Madame, I noticed a hotel with windows open on the first floor and a bistro below with outdoor seating. This was the perfect arrangement for a couple with a baby. Exhausted, we checked in and settled in a room on the first floor. We put Michelle to sleep on our portable crib mattress, which fit well in the back seat of our rented Renault, and also fit perfectly in the deep bottom drawer of an old armoire in our hotel room. With the upstairs windows open, we could enjoy a peaceful meal on the patio below while Michelle slept.

During most of our three-hour dinner that night, it seemed as if the chef was staring at us through the small window between the kitchen and dining room. I wondered if it were my imagination, but then Jorge asked why the chef appeared to be looking at us.

The student clientele from the nearby Sorbonne University had come and gone, but we lingered, happy to be able to relax a bit longer as Michelle slept and we enjoyed a glass of inexpensive house wine from the bottle on our bistro table. Eventually we noticed that we were the only ones left, so we started to get up to leave. Just then, the chef came to our table and asked about our nationality. Knowing that Americans were considered arrogant and loud due to the movie *The Ugly American,* we responded in our limited French that we were from Argentina.

The chef, Jean Claude, smiled and said he had a knack for determining the nationality of his clients, but admitted that we had confused him. We were right: He had been staring at us, trying to figure out where we were from. He noted that we were dressed like Americans, but used our utensils European-style. Jorge crossed his legs like a European man, knee over knee, whereas American men often rest the ankle of one leg on the knee of

the other. Believing that we were not Americans, Jean Claude began to tell us tales of American guests and tourists, including their strange eating habits and table manners. Our Christmas card that year revealed the fact that we were really Americans, but by then he was like family and it hardly mattered.

That first evening, our three-hour meal turned into six when Jean Claude and his lovely Russian wife, Jeanine, joined us at the table of his otherwise empty restaurant. The men enjoyed numerous glasses of Jean Claude's homemade liquor made from Mirabelle plums. Time stood still as we shared life stories and initiated what would become a lasting friendship. The *convivio* of that evening still draws our family to the corner of Rue de Madama and Rue de Fleurs every time we visit Paris, just as we had done with three-month-old Michelle.

Our families have remained close over the years. Michelle, while studying in Paris, lived with the Gramonds, and their son Marcel lived with us in Newport Beach, California. The family has cooked with us in California and Tuscany, and we have traveled through France together and stayed in their country home in Alsace. Our mutual love for *convivio* has led to a lifelong friendship, initiated because Jorge crossed his legs European style.

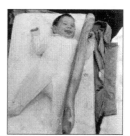

Michelle's first picnic at three months old, in Paris

When we finally arrived in England, the cuisine was disappointing. However, we did enjoy the cockles, which we bought by the pint, and good bacon and cheese became dietary staples.

The town of East Grinstead was a sleepy place where most people turned out the lights after dinner at six o'clock. That is, until we arrived. Jorge, still feeling the need to make a home-away-from home for lonely single doctors, made a habit of inviting them for dinner, sometimes on the same day he met them. Our rented home across the street from the hospital soon became the after-work hangout, and we once again made many new friends around our table.

One of our first guests, Juan Jose from Spain, became a regular. He had worked his way through medical school playing classical guitar professionally, and accustomed to the late dinner hours and nightlife of Spain, he'd had trouble adjusting to the silence of the evening in England. Nearly every night,

Juan Jose joined us for dinner and shared his talent. Michelle sat in awe of Juan Jose's guitar music and would eventually drift off to sleep while we enjoyed the evening. Our friendship led Jorge to share a medical practice with Juan Jose for a time in Valencia, Spain.

Our stay in England lasted only six months; we decided to return to the United States when I became pregnant again. In 1969, Jorge opened his first office in California and our son Jorge was born. Now with two children to feed, I continued doing as I had done with Michelle, providing small portions of whatever we had for dinner along with Michelle's favorites, bananas and sardines, once Jorge was ready for solid foods.

When Jorge and Michelle were still toddlers, just one and two years old, we had our third child, Jason. About the time Jason was ready for solid food, his paternal grandparents came to visit us from Argentina. I was pleased, but not at all surprised, when Jason's paternal grandmother fed him pureed table foods, just as she had done with my husband when he was a baby. This tradition would continue in our family. Some thirty-five years later, I heard Jason tell Jenn, his wife, that he wanted their kids fed only pureed adult food and no baby food. One day, his father-in-law told us how he had once telephoned his wife, who was babysitting Jason's nine-month-old son, Luca. He heard the baby's loud screams of discontent and asked what was wrong. Jason's mother-in-law screamed out, "He wants to eat and I can't get this damn blender to work!" So, the immigrant diet may actually live on in our family.

Food is tradition. Tastes and smells experienced in one's childhood are recalled in adult life. Taste may be physically sensed on the tongue and palate, but after it is cultivated, it becomes a distinct memory. If a baby is fed a bland diet and never experiences flavorful foods, that child will be deprived of one of the greatest pleasures of life. Healthy habits formed and nurtured during early childhood often last a lifetime.

I was fortunate to have my mother live with us when our children were in elementary school. She helped me carry on her Italian food culture with our own children. As a typical Italian grandma, she couldn't live without a garden, even though our house was in a Southern California suburb where private vegetable gardens were rare. Somehow Mom

managed to plant her tomatoes even before I could buy plants for my intended rose garden. Watching our children with her in the garden brought back happy memories of my childhood in Connecticut with my grandfather in his garden.

Fig trees are common in most Italian family gardens, and one day Mom asked me to bring her a fig tree for our California yard. Busy with three young children, I forgot her request. Sometime later, she asked me about the baby items stored in the garage and I told her that I had no plans to have more children and would give those things away someday.

Not long after that, I was parking the car in the garage when I noticed that my English baby pram and high chair were missing. When I asked Mom about this, she reminded me that the gardener's wife was pregnant and needed those things. She also reminded me that I had promised to get her a fig tree, informing me that she'd taken it upon herself to orchestrate a trade with the gardener. There, by the side of our suburban home, was a beautiful fig tree!

Years later, when we moved to our waterfront home in California, there was no room for a fig tree or a garden on our cement deck. Yet, a few months after our move, Mom presented me with some "homegrown" vegetables for our salad as I was making dinner. I had no idea where they had come from, but didn't think to ask. After dinner, Mom surprised me by taking me to her bedroom upstairs and out onto her private patio deck. Six feet up the side of the cement wall were rows of string beans, as well as pots of cherry tomatoes and peppers!

Just as my Italian parents had sometimes embarrassed me with their food culture and table rituals when I was growing up as "the Italian Girl," our children were mortified at times by our obsession with food and some aspects of our life around the table. It didn't take long after moving into our Newport home before we became known as "the Italian Family."

I'm not entirely sure how our family earned that name, but it probably originated with a clamming party organized by one of our neighbors. I immediately offered to bring homemade pasta when I heard about the party. I knew that making pasta for thirty neighbors wouldn't be any problem for me. There was just one challenge: How was I going to carry the pasta folded over two broomsticks down the street?

The answer was easy: I recruited my six-year-old daughter, Michelle. Together, we walked down to our neighbor's house, holding opposite ends of two broomsticks to keep the uncooked pasta aloft and intact. People driving by gave us funny looks, but that night was a great success. I made pasta for many parties after that, and this wonderful tradition eventually led me to offer pasta to the public as a way of sharing my passion and joy for cooking traditional foods.

When our children were old enough to begin school, I began noticing some real differences in the way our family ate. After school, most mothers would stop at the popular fast-food establishments for a treat with their children. The treats nearly always involved fries. My parents had ingrained in me a suspicion of outside food establishments, especially fast food, so I preferred to treat the kids to a *gelato*, Italian ice cream. Months later, we were all surprised (except, perhaps, for my own mother) to read how those tasty fries were actually cooked in refried animal fat. Then, upon discovering that some fast food establishments' tasty fries have some 18 ingredients, I saw mom was right. "Eat only what you know you are eating," she would say. At home our three ingredients are potatoes, oil and salt.

Concerns about their children's diets led mothers to turn to buying chicken nuggets, thinking this food would be a healthier choice for their kids. I'm sure they were horrified when, later on, the media began reporting on how much chicken skin and animal fat was inside each juicy nugget. These were not chicken pieces, but mysterious pseudo-chicken creations of the food industry. My Italian mother, like many others, would want to know what it was before feeding it to their children.

Taking our three children to see the play *Annie* in Los Angeles was one of those rare occasions when we ate out as a family—and provided yet more evidence that Jorge and I weren't raising our children according to the American parenting norm when it came to food. By that time, the children were nine, ten, and eleven years old.

My husband objected when the waiter tried to give our kids children's menus and insisted that the server give them regular menus. The children made their own selections and ate with gusto, which led me to wonder why American restaurants even provided children's menus. This wasn't the custom in Italy or France, or in many other countries. To eat right is like learning a language; the easiest way to learn is through total immersion, with parents setting the example.

My Argentinian in-laws also contributed when it came to encouraging our children to eat differently from their peers at school. For instance, the first time they visited us, my mother-in-law asked what time we were all having tea, and said she customarily had her *mate*, Argentinean tea, at four o'clock in the afternoon. I thought she was being unrealistic, offering a tea time to our children, considering they were only two, three. and four years old at the time. But, to my surprise, we all soon learned to enjoy tea time at four o'clock and had cheese and garlic bread to nibble on while seated at the table. It was unheard of in their family to nibble, eat standing away from the table, which was a great lesson for our children. They knew after our *merenda* there would be no snacks until dinner. Unfortunately, we failed to carry this lesson out later in life. As for the traditional Argentinian meal, it would be the *asado*, various meats cooked vertically over an open fire. I surprised Jorge for his fiftieth birthday with gauchos from Argentina who came to cook on the beach of Lido Isle with firemen in attendance since it was against the law. I begged for permission since some two hundred socialites were about to arrive for the event.

A few of our family food traditions weren't just different, but completely unacceptable in American culture. Once, while flying to Argentina when the kids were young, a flight attendant served the kids ice cream. Michelle requested "the yellow stuff" for the vanilla cup. The flight attendant looked at me.

Embarrassed, I quickly changed the subject. She would never understand how we occasionally topped our vanilla gelato with a few drops of the Italian liqueur Galliano. I am not advocating this other than to explain the food culture in our European upbringing.

When the neighborhood kids stopped by to play with our children, we often heard them make comments not about the food we were eating, but about the ritual of dining together. They'd complain to our children about it, saying, "Are you still eating?"

Whenever I suggested that these friends join us at the table, they'd usually say they had already eaten a taco or takeout food and weren't hungry. If they did join us, the other children never seemed able to eat as much as ours did, and often seemed to be full before the main course arrived. My husband guessed that this was most likely because of two reasons: They had probably been snacking after school, and they always consumed glasses of milk during the meal. My husband, like my mother, never allowed our children to drink milk at the dinner table, believing water was the best accompaniment, and was even better with a few drops of wine to color it a nice shade of pink.

Our drinking habits also raised questions, especially from neighbors whose children told them that we'd allowed them to drink wine with dinner. We quickly explained our philosophy and noted that the amount of wine never exceeded a drop or two in a glass of water. Our goal was to teach our children—as my father had taught my sisters and me—that alcoholic beverages should be enjoyed as a complement to foods rather than as a means to alter your mental state.

The drop turned to a half glass as the kids were in their teens, and eventually to a full glass of wine with dinner. It was very upsetting to my husband that we could not serve our children a sip of wine at our family table at our family restaurant as we could in Argentina or here in a restaurant in Italy.

A cold Heineken beer in our house always went well with a steaming bowl of homemade chili. A small shot of Sambuca liqueur enhanced our after-dinner espresso coffee. A robust red wine complemented our after-dinner cheeses. Of course, a few drops of Galliano liqueur over our vanilla ice cream made it extra delicious, even for an eight-year-old.

5

My Restaurant Table

"A crust eaten in peace is better than a banquet partaken in anxiety."

—AESOP

When my cousin Rocky and his family moved from Connecticut to join our family in California in 1975, Rocky needed a job. I suggested that we open a cuisine-to-go that specialized in pasta and sauces.

I had never dreamed of being a restaurateur. In the 1970s, being a chef was considered a dead-end job. Cooking certainly wasn't a popular career choice for women, especially for doctors' wives. As my mother-in-law said when I signed the lease for my first restaurant, "A doctor's wife can open a clothing boutique, but for heaven's sake, not a restaurant." We opened on Jason's sixth birthday, January 26, 1976. This was our staff, Grandma and our children. Nearly two decades later, we were still preparing food together.

In the 1970s, restaurant food culture was practically non-existent. Most customers weren't interested in the virtues of food quality and didn't pay much attention to the ingredients or the nutritional value of the dishes they ordered.

Still working together with Grandma years later

My initial attempt to change some of these general food habits and low standards began when Rocky and I started the What's Cooking Bistro. However, our concept didn't really enjoy great success until the 1980s, when eating more nutritiously and trying different dishes came into vogue. Brought up on the East Coast, I was familiar with many states that had neighborhoods of Italian immigrants where new arrivals were welcomed with a distinctive food culture as they adjusted to their new environment.

Southern California in the late 1960s lacked the "Little Italy" neighborhoods like those found across most of the eastern United States. In those neighborhoods, a good authentic Italian restaurant was easy to find. Newport Beach needed its own, and I was determined to open the first.

The search for a location led Rocky and me to the Irvine Company, the major landowner in the area. Company representatives told me about a strip mall being built on an open field of brush and weeds. It was a few miles from Fashion Island shopping center and up the street from the Harbor View neighborhood strip mall. At the time, it was hard to imagine a strip mall at that location, since there were few residences or commercial businesses in the area. The Irvine Company's real estate manager noted that food establishments generally failed in neighborhood strip malls. However, since I was inexperienced, I ignored this observation. I was just happy to have found a site, and accepted both the center's poor location at the end of a dead-end street and the lousy tenant space in the back corner of the mall. I wasn't even wise enough to bargain for a more visible location.

When my husband returned home from work every day, Jorge's habit was to greet me with a cheerful, "What's cooking?" This inspired our bistro's name. Rocky and I excitedly watched the Irvine Company's design plans develop. In 1976, after nine months of meetings, planning, permit approvals, and construction, we finally opened our doors.

We offered an exciting array of food items for the locals. However, the public wasn't ready yet for unfamiliar items like bean salads, cold pasta salads, veal dishes, or fresh oranges in wine. In 1976, I believe we were the only restaurant in Orange County to have a cappuccino machine and a panini press, as well as freshly made pasta and gnocchi. We were also one of the first places to offer frozen yogurt and gelato.

The public, accustomed to popular to-go menu choices like pizza, hamburgers, fried chicken, and french fries were initially unreceptive to our menu. The poor location certainly didn't help, especially since the Irvine Company had restrictions on signage. Diners looking for our location would end up at the Harbor View mall up the road, because they couldn't imagine that we might actually be located at the end of a desolate road.

Having lived in Paris with tables on the sidewalks, I found it difficult to understand why we couldn't have tables and chairs outdoors. Doing so would certainly make the center more inviting in our quiet little corner of the world.

However, my request for outdoor tables was rejected on the grounds that the tables might block pedestrian traffic. Days could go by without a single person walking past our location, except for an occasional curious grocery store shopper.

My requests to the Irvine Company for outdoor dining were unsuccessful, so I went to City Hall with my complaints and was rejected again.

When I saw a new tenant setting up his French coffee shop and placing a large umbrella and table outside, I returned to our landlord. How and why was he allowed to do so, when I was not? The Irvine Company representative said they were aware of the tenant's actions and had documented it in their file. I promptly suggested they make a note in my file, too, because I was going to put tables and chairs outside of my bistro. I never heard another word about it.

Having outdoor seating was an important first step toward getting people to notice our place. However, our challenges continued, and as our first year in business drew to a close, Rocky and I had to decide whether to stay or leave. Our tiny bistro of eight tables, barely two feet apart, couldn't cover our expenses. Having faith, we borrowed money and got bank loans to stay in business.

We watched new tenants in the center come and go, experiencing the same problems we did. When we got behind on rent, The Irvine Company was patient. Besides the market, our bistro was the only draw to the half-filled center during the day and the only one open after five o'clock. Even the original grocery store closed and was replaced by another. The French coffee shop with the umbrella outside its door also left. A plant shop disappeared during the night, as did a wine shop.

Fortunately, sponsoring events brought us lots of publicity. These events included dinners for the homeless, the Philharmonic Society, Alzheimer's groups, our church's building fund, Hoag Hospital, and various school and sports events.

As a member of the Pacific Opera board, I offered to have the after-opera dinner at our place, and had the privilege of serving our friend and my husband's compatriot, Placido Domingo, and other members of the opera cast. Our dinner ended at 5:00 a.m., which Placido said was customary in Spain.

We were pleased each time new tenants joined us in the center, and always dismayed when they left. I often considered leaving as well, but I had invested too much into our location. Things finally started to improve when we were discovered by the Ford Company, the closest major business in the area. Employees stood in line for the less-than-five-dollar lunch, knowing that our empanadas and pizzas, sold by the slice, came out of the oven at noon and sold as fast as we put them out.

Our lunch business with the Ford Company employees eventually led some to come back for dinner with their families.

Having to explain menu items to our customers helped me realize that some people weren't even familiar with the word "pasta." They seemed to know only one form of it: spaghetti, which they stereotyped as a high-calorie, hi-carb dish.

Cooking on the line with my cousin, I would run back and forth from the kitchen to the dining room to greet customers and answer questions about our menu. Why were some pasta dishes green? Why was the mozzarella so white? What are the black shells in this dish? Most had never experienced spinach pasta, *bufala* mozzarella, or a dish of pasta and mussels. Our espresso machine, purchased to meet the after-dinner needs of my husband and cousin, was also unfamiliar to most.

After working the line, I would do my office work as Rocky cleaned the kitchen. One night, I noticed that our most expensive purchase was cooking oil. I asked my mother and my cousin's wife, our only kitchen employees, about this, since our only fried item was *calamari fritti*. Mom explained that it was because our most successful takeout item, eggplant *parmigiana*, acted like a sponge. I needed to figure out a way to cut this expense, while at the same time making the dish healthier for customers. Most customers never considered how a dish is made, which is the reason most men would order a pasta dish such as *vongoli*, (about 300 calories) and the lady would select the eggplant, thinking it a better choice, not realizing it was probably our most caloric dish (about 750 calories). From that day on, we baked the eggplant slices in the oven. People happily continued to order the delicious and popular takeout tray for families and parties not realizing the change. This led me to decide to inform our customers of what they were eating, so I began sharing the caloric and nutritional ingredients of every menu item, as well as how each was prepared. I calculated the

calories and nutrients of each dish, using the list of ingredients taken from each recipe. I then compared the merits of our menu items to those of popular fast-food items, which at the time didn't disclose this information. I believe we were the first to do this.

Our updated menu was unusual enough in the 1980s to attract the attention of the *Daily Pilot.* They ran an article about our nutritional dishes, and compared a Big Mac and other fast food items to our pasta dishes. The article, "Pasta with a Slender Touch," noted that pasta's appeal should extend to those watching their waistlines. Our business increased a little following the newspaper's full-page coverage. Still, it was hard to convince everyone that a hamburger was not necessarily a better choice than pasta.

Shortly thereafter, the Pritikin diet became popular. Athletes realized that pasta was a good source of carbohydrate energy and began coming to our bistro from as far away as San Diego and San Francisco after reading about us in their local papers. We were totally unprepared for the crowds.

Our popularity continued to grow. After our first year in business, Rocky and his wife left for other endeavors. My dear mother remained in the kitchen, making twelve different kinds of pastas every day, using fresh spinach, beets, and carrots to add natural color and flavor. Using the ink from calamari, she even made black pasta, which was a hard sell at the time. I created daily sauces with fresh ingredients that our public had never experienced before. Pizza choices included whole wheat flour pizza, which was not accepted well at the time because it was the first time it was offered.

Real estate developers began appearing in the bistro regularly, offering us space in their upcoming shopping centers, and supermarket chains began requesting our products. I never considered expanding our operation to a bigger pasta-making enterprise because I rejected the idea of having to hire others to do the work and warehousing our products.

When one of our waiters wanted to try producing pasta for local businesses, however, I encouraged him to pursue the idea. He became successful in supplying restaurants with fresh pasta and eventually sold the business for a good profit.

I was also approached by a start-up company to help develop pasta that could be sold as a fast food to-go item in quart-sized containers. Once again, I considered the idea carefully, but rejected it. I couldn't see the feasibility of making pasta in a bucket without compromising quality. This business venture did fail, I understand.

Instead, our business took a different direction when the owner of Celestino's Market, an Italian meat market/deli in Newport Beach, asked me to supply him with fresh pasta. I questioned the idea of selling pasta in a meat market, but he claimed that some of his clients had suggested he carry it. I agreed to deliver twelve pounds of pasta the next morning. By afternoon, Celestino's Market had called to say that they had sold out and wanted an additional twenty pounds of pasta the next day. Demand continued to increase for our pastas and sauces from specialty shops in the area.

A supermarket chain approached me next, asking if we could give them the exclusive rights for our pastas and sauces, but I declined. I wanted to continue to be a hands-on operator. I looked forward to going to work, just as my father said it should be if you work all your life. Life at our restaurant rewarded me with joy. More importantly, I experienced *convivio* every day with family and friends.

I encouraged our clients requesting takeout pasta to cook it at home, since fresh pasta required only thirty seconds in boiling water. However, most customers still preferred cooked pasta. There are just seconds between properly made pasta *al dente* and overcooked pasta, so I understood their reluctance. In our restaurant, with so many orders coming in simultaneously, it was difficult at times to cook several orders on the few burners available. I couldn't find anything on the market that could solve my problem, so I designed a pasta cooker for multiple dishes: a pot with twelve cubicles of boiling water. The starchy water was drained out and fresh water was put into the cubicle, ready to heat up for the next dish. The quantity of water would be minimal, so that it could come to a quick boil and there would always be clean water for the next pasta order.

Our next-door neighbor did the design on paper for a prototype. I recall him commenting that when you think of something to invent, usually someone else in the world will be thinking of the same thing. I didn't take him too seriously. Pasta was gaining in popularity, but hadn't yet become the food craze of the 1980s. Then, while attending a medical meeting with my husband in Japan that year, we heard music coming from a nearby shopping mall in Tokyo. My husband's eyes were drawn to a balcony on the second floor, and he noticed a sign indicating a small bistro-type restaurant called Al Dente. Of course we had to check it out.

We were both stunned to see "my" pasta cooker in the middle of the kitchen! A customer seated at the bar noticed our shocked faces and asked if he could help. We asked about the multi-order pasta cooker, and after a quick phone call, the designer immediately came to meet us. Mr. Inoue Kousuke, vice president of the

R.R. Corporation, a division of Sony Corp., was very cordial. He said he knew little about pasta and sauces, but offered to do a deal. If I taught him about pasta, he would sell me the machines at cost. We became friends, often corresponding with each other and sharing pasta information. I was about to place an order when a U.S. company designed a pasta-cooking machine that met my needs. I never ordered a machine from Mr. Inoue, but our friendship continued for years. As our bistro business grew, I hired employees to cover the floor and work the line. Our hardworking dishwashers became our bistro cooks, and most employees remained with us for many years. People asked how I managed to find and retain such good employees. My system was to hire new employees for a two-week trial period, mostly to test their attitudes. Skills can be taught, but attitude is hard to change. Working long hours under pressure, the right attitude was especially important in a family-run operation. My dedicated staff was like family. They rarely quit, and I never needed to fire anyone.

My cooking staff worked diligently, kept their cool during stressful and hectic periods, never called in sick, and never came to work late. My waiters were Italian and created the right positive atmosphere on the floor, making everyone feel important the moment they entered our establishment. Many became regulars.

Only by working the line can one understand the challenges of a line cook. Servers yell their table orders. Customers demand special needs. Menu items change. Table orders go out simultaneously. Watching the speed and cooperation of our kitchen team reminded me of an opera performance. With an economy of movement, speed, and technique they performed their duties seamlessly. Our line cooks showed endurance and tolerance for the unexpected, knowing each day would bring new challenges.

Our staff seemed ready to serve in any capacity and always kept the business in mind. Late one evening, an employee in his trial period told a customer entering the restaurant that we were closed and to come back another time. My favorite dishwasher-turned-chef saw the disappointed faces of the late arrivals and came into the dining room, offering to heat up lasagna or an eggplant dish since the line was closed. The customers were very pleased. Besides running up a large check by consuming alcohol with their dinner, they became regulars and introduced their friends to our bistro.

Besides the regulars who came weekly, many came daily. I noted their likes and dislikes and often had food ready for them upon their arrival. A group of famous tennis pros came regularly. When they sat down at their table, I would have the server bring their bottles of cold beer before they even ordered. Smiles of gratitude followed.

People return to food establishments where they feel comfortable. Many authentic Italian restaurants thrive because they encourage their customers to enjoy *convivio* along with good food and fun. I hired a wonderful accordion player to play Neapolitan songs reminiscent of the old world during the dinner hours at What's Cooking. After a busy night, she would close the evening playing "Santa Ana" and the dining room staff and customers would sing along. At times they even danced, with the kitchen staff lined up with their utensils to accompany the music by banging on my collection of copper pots hanging between the kitchen and the dining room.

One particular night, a Greek couple said they believed Greeks are the only ones who enjoy life more than the Italians—only the Greeks could sing and dance while breaking dishes. That was all the challenge I needed. I went back to the kitchen and had our dishwasher find all the odd dishes, then asked Donna to play the music from the musical *Zorba the Greek*. I danced around and began to throw the dishes, accompanied by the music.

Off to Italy

Just then, my daughter and a date came through the bistro door. Shocked, Michelle ran up to help me, thinking I must be cracking up. When I explained that I was answering a challenge from a Greek couple, she laughed and said, "Mom, only you would do this!"

We created another great memory for ourselves and the staff in 1990, when the soccer World Cup took place in Italy. Knowing that our staff would probably have little interest in working during the games, I decided to take them all to Italy where, along with the excitement of the games, they could experience *convivio* in Italy for themselves.

Uncle John with Jason and Jorge

Our family worked hard to bring cheer to the dining experience, being informal yet doing things with class, even organizing parties in our little, unknown center. Once, for instance, we invited two hundred customers for an outdoor gourmet dinner with a string quartet. My novel idea was well received. My talented brother-in-law, John Sambuco, a violinist with the Minneapolis Symphony Orchestra, had his own quartet who volunteered to perform. The music was fabulous, the evening was fantastic, and our food was delicious. We purchased over two hundred potted yellow plants to decorate the center and invited all of our guests to take home a plant, being that Irvine Co. said they did not have a budget to beautify the center at the time. Rumor had it that they had intentions of closing it down. Being as we were the only stable tenant, they didn't care if rent was a month or two behind. "Just don't leave us," we were told. Soon after, our success brought even longer lines to the door of our small bistro.

6

Expanding *Convivio* in California

"We should look for someone to eat and drink with
before we look for something to eat and drink."

—Epicurus

Our success in selling fresh pasta at the meat market and the requests from customers to open another establishment led me to search for a second location. At the time, the 17th Street area on the border of Newport and Costa Mesa had plenty of parking and was close to many other businesses catering to a great clientele. We found a yogurt shop going out of business in that area and decided to lease the space. The size was perfect, since we could use our larger kitchen at the bistro to supply this location with our specialties. More than fast food take-out, but not quite a restaurant, the concept for our new venture, What's Cooking Express Cuisine, suited our growing community of quality food lovers. We even added a rotisserie so customers could enjoy daily specials and order fresh meats in advance.

While busy converting the yogurt shop into our new kitchen, my sisters, Rose and Mary, bought a Kentucky Fried Chicken location in Dana Point. Mom and my sisters worked hard to make it a successful franchise. This resulted in an unusual visit from the Colonel himself to meet the ladies and determine the reason for their great success. He paid special attention to Mom, who enjoyed every minute of his visit.

Working at their Kentucky Fried Chicken franchise, my mother and sisters noticed a restaurant nearby that had gone out of business. The building was now available for lease.

I wasn't interested in expanding again because I was already in the process of building out our second location. Nevertheless, at their urging, I drove twenty minutes south one day to check it out. The space was gloomy and smelled like a moldy cellar full of overripe cheese. I told my sisters this, and explained that it wasn't feasible for me to open another restaurant at this time. They encouraged me to look at the space again. It did look a little better during the day. After a few more visits, I could envision the potential for a third location. I signed the lease and launched our first dinner house, Luciana's, in 1981. The restaurant was well received by locals and visitors alike.

Over the years, we continued to hold a variety of charity events at all three of our locations. These benefits raised donations for local organizations and national charities. Our most successful event was a dinner at Luciana's for Augie's Quest, an organization raising funds to find the cure for ALS./ Lou Gehrig's Disease. We're proud to have raised $65,000 that night for our friend Augie Nieto's charity.

As if owning and managing three food establishments in California wasn't enough, within a few years, my life became even more complicated following a visit to Italy.

In January 1985, while chatting with an Alitalia airlines pilot after dinner at Luciana's, my husband mentioned that I was on my way to Italy the next morning to attend a food conference. I mentioned my desire to fix up an old country home someday. Before leaving, the pilot handed me a note with the name and phone number of his good friend Fabio, a realtor in Florence. I certainly wasn't interested in buying real estate in Italy, I told him, and explained that I was already overcommitted.

While packing up at the end of the conference, however, I found the pilot's note with Fabio's number and decided that sending regards from his friend warranted a call. We had a nice lunch the next day, and Fabio offered to show me a country house he was selling, one that was all but abandoned. I said no, but thanked him for a most superb gourmet *pranzo*.

I couldn't fall asleep that night, wondering if I might have missed a great opportunity. I called Fabio the next morning and said I'd like to see the property after all.

As we drove out to the house, Fabio explained that the oldest member of the family owned the property and only used the five-hundred-year old structure occasionally. Whenever he needed peace and tranquility away from the city, this man would wander around the fifteen-acre olive grove and take in the views of the rolling Tuscan hills. When the weather turned foul, he sought shelter in the old farmhouse with a leaky roof. I fell in love with the story of the old man and with the old house too, which led me to put down a deposit to secure the property despite worrying about what Jorge would say or even if the check was covered. When I arrived home from Italy, Jorge looked up from his newspaper, noticed my small carry on, and asked me why I hadn't bought anything since the dollar exchange was so good.

"I actually did," I said.

"Then it must be very small," he said.

"No, it's so big that I left it there," I answered.

I was emptying my suitcase when curiosity propelled Jorge into our bedroom.

"What in the world did you buy?" he asked.

I knew what his response would be, so I gave him a hug, told him I had missed him, then said, "I bought a house." He laughed, knowing that I had to be kidding.

As he was leaving the room, I called, "I *did*."

Jorge's Latin outrage immediately emerged full force. "Are you out of your mind?" he shouted.

I reassured him that I was not, and said that I wasn't sure if we had the funds, but I had written a check on Friday, knowing I would have time to either cancel the deposit or cover it. Jorge was relieved to hear this. Unfortunately, the next day the Italian bank informed me that you can't just write a check and cancel it like you can in America.

Little did I know that my impulsive two-thousand-dollar deposit was going to result in me committing the next thirty-five years of my life to working on a farm in Italy.

Italian and French Culinary Differences

"In our society, there is a fear of food that brings about the fear of pleasure."

—Julia Child

As I realized during my travels in Italy, eating is done joyfully in that country, typically with family and friends at the table. Americans eat when we're hungry, or even when we're not, any place, any time, and often alone. We deprive ourselves of an authentic and intimate dining experience, and when my friends from Italy visit, they often comment on this.

During a taxi ride in New York City with my husband and an Italian visitor, Silvio, for instance, the taxi driver asked if he could make a quick stop with the meter off to pick up a sandwich. Silvio couldn't understand how anyone could eat in a car. Was the cab driver so busy that he couldn't make time to stop and eat? I did not mention to Silvio that thirty percent of the population in America eats at least once a day in their vehicles, thanks to cars equipped with beverage holders and portable foods like chicken nuggets, burritos, and fries.

Later, we saw a group of mothers walking their kids to school. Silvio was mystified when he observed that they were all carrying big coffee cups and their children were eating croissants as they walked. "Do they enjoy eating while walking?" Silvio asked, adding, "In Italy, you may go for a walk after dinner with an ice cream cone, but not sandwiches, fruits, and croissants."

Silvio then proceeded to tell me how he ended his relationship with an American girl due to food culture. My surprise led to his explanation of the importance of *pranzo*, the midday meal, and how it can be a sensuous pleasure. His ex-girlfriend did not like food and had almost a fear of it. Now I was completely at a loss until he compared eating to lovemaking—both should be done slowly so as to enjoy each step as well as intimacy with a loved one. My thoughts were, "Who has time midday?" He explained how he disliked what was happening in many cities, particularly historical centers such as Florence, his hometown, where popular mom-and-pop trattorias had been transformed into fast food establishments.

Francois, a friend recently visiting from France, conveyed a similar sentiment about the once-popular brasseries and classic cafés of Paris having become burger and pizza joints serving tourists, regrettably affecting the tradition of the leisurely afternoon meal at the table. I had to agree with both men because unfortunately it was true. By disrupting the traditional habit of a leisurely lunch, one can easily be led to adopting the habit of snacking to replace meals. There is a correlation between snacks replacing meals and the increase in obesity today in both France and Italy. Partly responsible is the establishments of fast-food locations serving food all day. With the increase in locations every year, Italy is beginning to show the consequences of the adoption of fast food. As my friend Francois stated, "Why can't Americans adopt our eating habits instead of us adopting theirs?"

Following my suggestion that Silvio give his friend time to experience his culture, he responded that the degree of difference in food culture was too great to overcome and he continued to relate eating to lovemaking. If one has the time, and work allows it, nothing can compare to lovemaking after a sensuous lunch with a great bottle of wine and a short nap. He could never adapt to a lifestyle of ordering fast food from the car window and eating it on the run. This brought to mind a quote by Jean Brillat-Savarin, the French lawyer and politician, who stressed in his book, *The Physiology of Taste,* the importance of the pleasure of the table. He refers to daily life at the table as a sensuous experience, a time to enjoy the moment. He claims a little bit of grape juice helps. "Burgundy makes you think of silly things, Bordeaux makes you talk about them, and Champagne makes you do them."

"The art of eating gives sensuality to live life," Silvio continued. "One must not just read the menu, but digest it." I had to agree that the separate dishes that make up the Italian *pranzo* gave one time to digest and enjoy each morsel, but never thought of it as sensual. He commented on a buffet he experienced with Shirley at a California social event. People piled food high on their plates, as if in preparation for their last meal, with the flavors all mixed together. They could not distinguish one flavor from another as they tried to balance plate and wine glass while standing and carrying on a conversation. I recall my husband refusing to eat that way. He would return home for dinner after social events serving buffets. He disliked, as did Silvio, buffets requiring one to stand and eat and socialize, something he had never experienced in Argentina. He felt that by crowding the plate with a mélange of items, one could not enjoy and savor each item. Time between servings also allows for better digestion and absorption of nutrients and a more enjoyable and lengthy dining experience.

Silvio was convinced that life with Shirley would not provide the future he was looking for. Shirley, raised by a single working mother who depended on prepared foods and fast food to feed her daughter, rarely experienced a home-cooked meal and over time adopted an unhealthy relationship with food. She would diet, starve herself, binge, take pills and even avoid sitting down for a meal. He feared that if they had children, they would never have the experience of smelling the aromas of a home-cooked meal, know the tastes and smells of the kitchen, or enjoy the conviviality of eating at leisure with family and friends. Never before did I consider that differences in food culture could be a factor in dissolving a relationship.

Silvio wasn't a member of the Slow Food Movement, started in Bra, a small town in the Piedmont region of Italy, but his views echoed that of its founder and president, Carlo Petrini, a journalist. The Slow Food Movement was organized by a group of fun-loving men as a way to promote a new philosophy of dining and stop the advances of fast food. Petrini and his small group started what is now a worldwide organization with about one hundred thousand members in over fifty countries. They have over thirteen hundred chapters, referred to as *Convivia*.

Members of the Slow Food movement try to spread the word that there is a correlation between snacks replacing meals and the increase of obesity. Fast food locations serving food all day are partly responsible; it's easy to see the effects of these places, which have recently made headway in Europe. The first McDonald's built in Europe was in Germany in 1971. France followed quickly in 1972, but Italy managed to hold out until the mid-1980s, about the time I bought the Tuscan farmhouse.

Italians unaccustomed to patronizing fast-food establishments fought hard to stop the outlets from coming into Italy, especially to beautiful tourist attractions like Piazza di Spagna in Rome. Area residents complained about the smell of fried food. Designers, including Valentino, fought hard with a lawsuit.

McDonald's fought back. They improved their air vents and, when the city complained about the added rubbish, McDonald's improved their trash collection system. The Italians also complained about the stigma of globalization associated with the culture and lifestyle of the United States, which they didn't want to adopt. Despite valiant efforts, however, nothing the Italians did could stop the tourists and students from abroad from buying the economical, familiar McDonald's food.

The acceptance of McDonald's was initially slow. However, the opportunity for growth came in the mid-1980s, when McDonald's partnered with Cremonini, the largest Italian meat producer. Cremonini is known for its quality farm-to-table products and has many outlets, from restaurants to *autogrills*. They also owned an American- style hamburger establishment called Burghy.

Eventually, McDonald's executives learned that to expand their business throughout Italy, they needed to step up the quality of their menu items. Buying Italian products was a critical first step, so McDonald's struck a deal: if Burghy sold them all of their locations, McDonald's would agree to buy their meat exclusively from Cremonini. This was a win-win business deal for both parties. It allowed McDonald's to establish itself successfully in Italy, where other fast-food establishments had failed, and it gave Cremonini the exclusive for their meat products. Unfortunately, with the increase in the number of fast-food locations like McDonald's every year, Italy is beginning to show the consequence of the adoption of fast food: an increase in obesity.

With a snail as its logo, The Slow Food Movement educates consumers about the risk of fast food, encourages ethical buying in local markets, and highlights the importance of conviviality, the core of the slow food philosophy. As a member of Slow Food, I have attended chapter meetings in Tuscany and Abruzzo, where they discussed and served genuine foods and encouraged time at the family dinner table. Not strange to me, desert was not offered after a most delicious meal. It is not the important course it is in America.

France and Italy may have similar food cultures, but they were born out of different histories. Following the French Revolution, the nobility no longer needed French chefs in their households. Unemployed chefs opened bistros and restaurants to practice their culinary skills, and eating out became popular in France. In 1789, there were fewer than one hundred restaurants in Paris. Fifteen years later, there were over five hundred. With this proliferation came the uncertainty of culinary rules and codes. The nouveau riche cuisine needed guidance and direction. French chefs like Escoffier established strict culinary rules and codes.

In early civilizations, such as in France and China, aristocracy played an important role in the kitchen. Chefs created cuisines of innovative dishes to meet the needs of the imperial courts for some one thousand years, as well as meeting the needs of wealthy patrons. The aristocracy created *haute cuisine*. French chefs learned classic cuisine, beginning their training as early as the age of twelve. They learned exact measurements and recipes from their chef mentor. That is why recipes may be similar, with few modifications from one bistro to another. *Haute cuisine* failed in England in spite of its elaborate thousand-year monarchy because it was difficult to develop a sophisticated cuisine in her cold climate. With poor quality ingredients, there was little innovation or creativity forcing England to adopt the cuisines of other nations.

Italy, on the other hand, had no permanent central monarchy, and lacked a national cuisine of aristocrats. The owners of Italian trattorias picked up their culinary skills in the family kitchen and learned to cook as their grandmas did. Families came from different regions of Italy, cut off from one another, so their mothers and grandmothers taught them how to use what was available in their areas. Italian food today comes from the peasants' food of yesterday, rather than that of grand chefs.

The mama and papa cooks were not graduates of culinary schools. They were often farmers, yet they taught the aristocracy what to eat and how to prepare it. Today, cultures desiring to return to the land need only turn to Italy. Italy never gave up the desire for seasonal, natural, and healthy foods. Italy's heart is still on the farm.

Because for years the twenty regions of Italy were cut off from one another, Italy's amazing variety of artisan foods explains why popular Italian dishes like lasagna or minestrone vary from region to region, and even from town to town. Central regions make lasagna with meat sauce. Northern areas make it with cream sauce. Liguria makes it with pesto sauce. The south uses ricotta. In Sicily, lasagna refers to the wide noodle served without layering sheets of pasta. All of these dishes are lasagna, and each region considers its version to be the true, the best lasagna. Every region also has its own version of minestrone soup, using ingredients available in their regions: Liguria adds pesto, Naples adds pasta, Milano adds rice, Tuscany adds beans, and coastal areas add fish.

Even today, in spite of improved communications and transportation, most Italians remain loyal to their region, resulting in an amazing variety of artisan food specialties. *Campanilismo*, referring to the church bell tower, signifies Italians' strong connection to their particular town. Attachment to the town square is often for culinary reasons, signifying their gastronomical emblem. They eat what they produce locally, and what tradition dictates, since it is a matter of their reputation and pride.

Italy produces more types of cheese and wine than any other country in the world, too, because each region, province, town, and even family has its own specialties. Cheeses commonly used in cooking, such as mozzarella, *parmigiana*, and ricotta are exported in great volume. There are thousands of delicious artisan cheeses made from unpasteurized sheep and goat milk. Many of these unpasteurized products aren't allowed to be imported into the U.S., so Italy is the only place to experience such a variety of unique flavor profiles.

Besides being the largest producer and exporter of wine, Italy is the only country that produces wine in every region. The seemingly endless varieties are mainly due to the varying climates, terrains, and soil qualities. Local methods of production vary. Italians usually do not add sulfites unless they are required for exporting. In addition *prosecco*, an Italian product, has become the most popular sparkling wine in the world, outselling French champagne.

Another similarity between the French and the Italians is that as southern Europeans, they have a different drinking culture than their northern European neighbors. Because they are wine-producing nations, their citizens drink socially but in moderation. The people of Northern Europe consume more hard liquor and beer, often leading to binge drinking.

There are differences between the two wine-producing nations. The French drink five times more than the Italians and believe drinking benefits their virility. The Italians do not share this idea. They do not tolerate heavy drinking or find it amusing. In Italy, it is a personal disgrace for a family member to become inebriated. Dr. David J. Hanson, an expert in the study of alcoholism and cultural differences, has written a study titled, "Italian Teens Frown on Binge Drinking." He discusses how the Italians do not have a culture of intoxication. When families allow wine with meals, one is less likely to develop harmful drinking problems as an adult.

The differences between intoxication and non-intoxication cultures has led to many studies. Of particular interest are those on youth drinking behavior by Margaretha Järvinen and Robin Room, as well as those by F. Beccaria and OV Guidoni, who discuss the differences in drinking and drunkenness among nations back to Roman times. Margaretha Järvine cites in one study the Roman historian Tacitus, who stated that the German lifestyle contrasted considerably with the civilized lifestyle of the Romans. In classical times, he was referring to the German tribal groups of northern nations: Norway, Sweden, Finland, Denmark, Iceland, Germany, Austria, England, and Scotland. He explained that they believe "drinking bouts lasting days and nights are not considered in any way disgraceful."

Martin Luther was quoted as complaining about the "abuse of eating and drinking by the Germans," again referring to what were at the time tribal groups of Northern Europe. The Nordic country adolescents also drank frequently and often to intoxication, as their parents do. Luther expressed how "Italians call us gluttonous drunken Germans and pigs because they live decently and do not drink until drunk." The Italians drink wine at the table with their meal to be social, not to become intoxicated.

An English traveler and contemporary of Luther, Fynes Moryson, confirmed his beliefs when stating that the northern countries, "to their drinking they can prescribe no means nor end." The Scandinavians and the Finns he portrayed as "proud and self-willed people with a tendency to go berserk when drinking alcohol." Like the British, the Nordic adolescents drank as a social step towards adulthood and maturity. This is the opposite for the Italian adolescent, who by choosing to abstain or to drink responsibly shows maturity and good judgment. Parents have influence and those with a non-intoxication drinking culture are better role models for their children. These studies conclude that the upbringing of children, parental attitudes, and family relationships are factors related to adolescents' drinking behavior. For Italians, wine is to be consumed socially and with food.

Although youth alcoholism continues to be less prevalent in the wine-drinking nations, differences between nations are becoming less evident with globalization. This is having detrimental effects on behavior and culinary culture. The Mediterranean moderate drinking culture is being challenged. In Italy, seeing the increase of pubs competing with the Italian-style coffee bars has had an effect on its drinking culture. Victorio Sgarbi, an art critic provocateur, Minister of Italian Culture, a counselor of the Milan City Council, and once mayor of the wine producing city Salemi has a solution in Sicily, which demonstrates the Italian mentality regarding drinking. He encourages youth to continue to drink wine stating, "We have to teach young people to drink wine. If there is something to ban, it is Coca-Cola, Fanta and other disgusting products. I invite all young people to Salemi to drink freely."

Southern Italy is most likely where the Mediterranean diet originated. Pellegrino Artusi, in his *La Scienza in Cucina e l'Arte di Mangiar Bene (Science in the Kitchen and the Art of Eating Well)* published in 1891, refers to the importance of the Mediterranean diet in his hugely successful cookbook. He based a healthy diet on grains, vegetables, wine, and olive oil. This is where the seed of the Mediterranean diet began, when poverty and good health existed side by side.

Creativity is very important in Italian cuisine, especially when having to depend on inexpensive ingredients. I have experienced some of the best cuisine in Italy made from some of the least expensive ingredients. Artusi believed food should be judged by its merits, not its cost, and accentuated the importance of conviviality of the table, saying, "To invite someone is to be responsible for his happiness, as long as he is under your roof." This is very much the Italian philosophy, even today.

Another notable feature of Italian food culture is that when it comes to food, Italy is a true democracy. Food is the common language, accessible to all regardless of income. Italy's culinary code is the glue that unifies the nation. After winning the World Cup in soccer, the Italians filled the neighborhood coffee bars singing, eating, and celebrating their victory with food, rather than with alcohol.

Nobody can truly understand Italy without first cracking that culinary code. As the modern world encroaches, Italians are often critical of those who fail to follow what they believe to be the correct way. This might include missing the ritual of lunch, having coffee or soda during a meal, having tea or cappuccino after a meal, serving unsuitable wine, or indulging in spirits before a meal.

Francois, my dear Parisian friend, agrees that the influence of modern life has been more detrimental to the French food culture than to Italian food culture. Working parents, busy schedules, a profusion of eating possibilities on each corner, and vending machines with poor-quality snacks reflect how France has unfortunately been mirroring the United States since the late 1980s.

This made France an easy target for foreign chains: McDonald's from the U.S., a fast-food hamburger chain from Belgium, kebab stands from Turkey, and recently, pasta-to-go from Italy. France's pasta-to-go, as I experienced it, was a two-minute microwave product sold for three Euros. It was dreadful.

Globalization is endangering Italy's gastronomical culture, too. Like France and most other industrialized nations, the Italian homemaker is increasingly a thing of the past, as more Italian women work full-time. Italians are starting to take shortcuts to feed their families and are moving away from the food traditions practiced by their mothers and grandmothers. If this continues, sadly, future generations may never get to appreciate the richness of the old-world kitchen.

Our desire to introduce our children to cultures around the world, even within a limited budget, led me to organize exchanging visits for our children with visits for the children of Jorge's medical colleagues. For example, Michelle at age twelve enjoyed a summer in Caracas, Venezuela, as we enjoyed hosting Doctor Ochoa's two daughters.

In 1981, a trip we had planned to take to Europe fell through due to my father-in-law's health issues. He was visiting us from Argentina and needed medical attention and surgery not covered by insurance in America. This presented us with some unplanned expenses, and led to canceling our summer travel plans. I was disappointed, but given my Italian DNA, I knew I'd find an arrangement—an "*arrangero*," as they say.

Coincidentally, I noticed an ad in our local paper for a "Home Exchange." I presented the idea to Jorge that evening, but he wouldn't even consider having a strange family living in our home for the summer. I tried to explain that I was sure they would respect our home as we would theirs, but he refused to discuss it.

The next day, I sent away for the literature on the advertised home anyway, driven by my excitement about a beautiful country estate in Rambouillet, France, with a swimming pool and tennis court being available, along with an apartment in the Place des Victoires in Paris. No way was I going to miss this opportunity!

The following week the pictures arrived, showing the exchange home on the cover of a French home designer's magazine. I spread the pictures out on our dining room table so they would be impossible to miss. My husband viewed them and, not knowing why they were there, commented on the beauty of the country estate in France.

As Jorge enjoyed a glass of Vermouth, I prepared his favorite dish, *pasta con vongole*. When I noticed he was in a good mood, I presented my idea. Again, he rejected it. Knowing him well, I quickly changed the subject. That night as we were going to bed, Jorge repeated that he would have no part in this exchange. If I really wanted to do it, I would have to do it myself. I responded that I would think about it.

At breakfast the next morning, Jorge asked if I were to go to France with the children, where would he live? "You might just have to come with us," I replied with a smile.

As the home exchange would be for only four weeks, I needed to find an inexpensive way to have a longer stay in Europe with our children. I did some research and found religious lodgings in Europe that would accept only women and children for a meager fee of about five dollars a day. This would be a good opportunity for our children to learn the value of the dollar and the importance of speaking other languages, I decided. My plan worked: Without having to sleep outdoors, we managed to backpack our way through some six countries in Europe for five dollars a day.

During our European travels, Jorge had remained in California to orient the French family upon their arrival to our Newport Beach home. I arranged for the children to extend their stay for a few weeks by attending the American International School in Lugano, Switzerland, while I went on to France to see exactly what I was getting our family into.

The moment I saw the ivory-covered outer walls of the house in France, I felt at home. Our host, Emma, arranged a wonderful barbecue to introduce me to the neighbors and showed me the area and the activities available for the family. I was very surprised to see about fifteen lovely French women of all ages and sizes, topless, walking around the grounds and sitting by the pool. After changing into my conservative one piece, Emma suggested that I lower the straps of my bathing suit, so as not to have strap marks. I informed her that I thought it was actually a good idea for my husband to find those strap lines on my soon-to-be tanned body when he arrived. When Emma asked if she could be topless in Newport Beach, I surprised her with a definitive, "No."

Feeling out of place in my modest suit, I avoided staring at the topless bodies by concentrating on the long thin leg of lamb on the barbecue.

As mealtime approached, I went to the kitchen to help Emma prepare salads and other vegetable dishes while Jean Franco, her husband, went outside to cut the lamb. The food was set out on the patio, family-style, with paper-thin slices of lamb spread out on a platter surrounded by a cornucopia of fresh seasonal vegetables. I was surprised to see that there was no other meat option, and couldn't help comparing the small portions of meat for a party to the way our family of five could consume an entire leg of lamb in California.

The next morning, Emma stayed home from work to be with me. I noticed there was no breakfast prepared, and she told me that we would go out for café lattes at her favorite café. The doorbell rang, and I quickly figured out our café visit would have to wait. Emma moved a few chairs and her sofa to the wall and introduced me to her personal trainer, who gave us a thirty-minute stretching class, which included a few good yoga positions.

After he departed and the furniture was returned to its proper places, we went out for our café lattes. Emma ordered two croissants with our lattes. I couldn't help but feel guilty devouring the sweet specialties, but Emma explained that she would never deprive herself of her morning croissant. It was her special treat of the day, and she would rather cut out a piece of bread at dinner than miss her breakfast ritual. This was her time to enjoy watching people, visiting with friends, and glancing over the morning paper. My Italian friends also do not deprive themselves of this treat.

Emma worked in her husband's commercial real estate office, but managed to have lunch ready for her family at 1:30 each day. Both mornings I was there, she spent no more than half an hour preparing the lunch meal ahead. Upon arriving home at 1:00 p.m., she needed only to complete the final steps. That first morning, she chopped vegetables and sautéed chicken and left them ready to go into the oven when she returned home. I had no idea that she was preparing a fantastic French chicken fricassee, known as coq au vin.

When her children returned from school for lunch, Emma put her morning prep into the oven for its remaining thirty-minute cooking time. She had thirteen-year-old Anita rub the salad bowl with a few cloves of garlic, while fifteen-year-old Claudio set the table. Jean Franco read the paper and discussed some of the current events with the family. While the meal cooked in the oven, Emma helped Anita with her homework as Claudio sat with his dad and discussed the summer Olympics. In less than thirty minutes after returning home, a delicious hot meal was on the table.

Having that two-hour break during the day gave this family quality time together and time to catch up with each other's doings. They all took part in clearing the table and doing the dishes. During that first lunch with the family, Anita told me about a new McDonalds that had just opened. I asked her whether she thought it would become popular, and she said that she and her friends might try it out of curiosity, but felt that if you have a good meal waiting for you at home, a Big Mac would not be very tempting. Of course, that was over thirty years ago. Today, there are close to 1,700 outlets. I am not sure if Anita ever learned to appreciate the fast food establishment, but she may be part of the last generation not to do so.

My family enjoyed every minute in our exchange home. Meanwhile, Emma's family kept our neighbors thoroughly entertained in Newport Beach. The normally quiet bay had a traffic jam of boats in front of our dock. Apparently, everyone was enjoying our topless sunbathing house guests. When I called to apologize to our recently-divorced neighbor, he explained there was no need to be sorry, and said Emma had asked him if the women could sunbathe topless. He had told them, "Sure, go right ahead." Upon our return, our neighbors booed us and asked when we were bringing back the French!

During our stay in Rambouillet, our good friend, the Parisian chef Jean Claude, invited us to join his family in a region of Lorraine, in the northeast corner of France. Every day, Jean Claude would go out with us to pick mushrooms to complement the evening meal. We also fished for trout, and I went for walks with his wife, Jeanine, while our husbands killed a rabbit or chicken for dinner.

My house gift to our hosts was a pasta machine from Italy. As Michelle said, "Only my mother would bring a pasta machine to a famous French chef and give a pasta-making class the next day."

I promised Jean Claude that the students patronizing his restaurant would love it, as pasta was quickly becoming the food of the eighties. Initially, he would have no part of it, saying, "Great chefs trained at Maxim's in Paris do not make pasta." Nonetheless, I convinced him to try it, and it turned out to be a fun day for all.

How fortunate we were to be able to experience *convivio* with our friends in their country home. I'll never forget that time, when we were served daily by a French chef whose specialties included potatoes of Breux, *pâté*, Lorraine of pork, veal baked in pastry, rabbit au vin with wild morels (picked that morning), trout on the grill (fished out of his lake the same day), *andouille* sausages made of tripe, and Jean Claude's homemade Mirabelle plum wine.

After this introduction to Europe, the children were eager to return the following year. Michelle spent part of the summer with a French family in Pau, on the northern edge of the Pyrenees. Afterward, she wanted to stay in France longer. My husband and I explained that she couldn't unless she worked, and given the unemployment statistics for youth in France, as well as their unfavorable opinion of American youth at the time, that would be impossible. I agreed to join her for her last week.

Upon my arrival at the airport, however, I realized that my daughter had inherited the Italian DNA of *arrangiamento*: Michelle had managed to find employment as a host in a restaurant in the Montparnasse area. The fact that she was proficient in four languages surely helped. It worked out better than I could have planned; now we could both enjoy another a month in Paris together.

Shortly after my arrival, Michelle and I decided to make a surprise visit to Che Gramond's Bistro. The moment we entered, Jean Claude and Jeanine jumped out of their seats and greeted us with hugs and kisses. They insisted that we stay for lunch, but we respectfully declined so as not to interfere with the business.

Jean Claude refused to take no for an answer. He quickly put a "Closed" sign in the window and told us to meet him in front of the restaurant, since we were staying in our usual hotel next door where Michelle had slept in the bottom drawer of an armoire as a three-month-old.

An hour later, we were enjoying the scenery of the Champagne countryside from the windows of Jean Claude's car: vineyards, old farmhouses, and medieval villages encircling lovely churches. Eventually, he stopped at a winding creek with colorful flowers carpeting its banks so we could take a walk. Jeanine took out an old leather shoulder bag. As Michelle and I walked with her along the river bank, she removed from her bag a little metric ruler explaining it was to measure the fish she would catch before putting them in her sack. I soon realized she had planned to fish along the creek. She explained how government officials would often come and check on the size of the fish to be sure that those under a certain size would be released back into the creek.

Back at the car, Michelle and I were surprised to see that Jean Claude had set up a little folding picnic table, four chairs, and place settings. There were even four crystal wine glasses. Jeanine gave him a hand at removing a straw picnic basket, which had foie gras made by Jean Claude, freshly baked country bread, vegetable quiche, fruit, and a colorful wicker basket filled with a variety of French cheeses. His face glowed with happiness as he sang in French, "Long live the Monarchy" while opening one of his favorite wines, a Pomerol of the Bordeaux region, stored for some fifteen years in his underground wine cellar. Following our picnic Jeanine wandered off to the bank to fish as Michelle settled down on the bank to read the life history of Jim Morrison of The Doors rock band.

I remained with Jean Claude to enjoy the last drops of the superb velvety Petrus, a second bottle that had been removed that morning meters below his restaurant in the Sixth Arrondissement.

I asked him why he did not buy a little cottage in the woods since he loved it so much. His answer, I shall never forget, was, "Then I would live like you Americans, spending your weekends taking care of the plumbing, yearly painting, and cleaning." His comment, I realized, resulted from an experience he had when he came with us to our mountain home in Lake Arrowhead while visiting us in California. At that time, I had mentioned that we never seemed to have time to use our vacation home, due to our busy schedule, other than to drive up to take care of it. I realized he had a point when he added that the entire countryside was free. We can come every week to a different spot to enjoy the beauty of nature without the headaches. It took us two years, but his comments eventually led to the sale of our A-framed cottage in the woods, which we rarely used.

Needing a place to stay for the month, I had jumped at the opportunity when Jean Claude told me about a one-room rental above his restaurant. The building was once the home of American prose writer Gertrude Stein; when I had dinner in the evenings, I often thought about what it must have been like when Stein entertained artists and writers here, including Hemingway, Picasso, and Matisse.

While Michelle was busy working, I had opportunities to cook with Jean Claude in his little restaurant kitchen. The space was so constrained that I was always amazed by what he could create from the fresh products kept in baskets outside the kitchen door. Best of all, Jean Claude invited me to accompany him to the largest wholesale market in the world, Rungis. This was a special invitation, since only authorized clients could enter this unique indoor market, where chefs and traders from all over Europe buy and sell every day.

This rare invite meant meeting Jean Claude downstairs at 3:30 a.m. for the half-hour drive to Rungis. The market was only open until 7:00 a.m., so it was important to arrive early for the best selection.

We entered the hall of fish when we arrived, where I heard the vendors explaining the history and quality of each fish. Jean Claude purchased some scallops, explaining that the only way to be sure it was a real scallop was to see it in its full form. Clever salesmen can cut cheap white fish into circles, and if not cognizant of the taste, buyers can be fooled. He preferred scallops caught by divers, more delicate, and not dredged. Dredgers take longer to deliver to market and the result is a sandier scallop. Buying tuna, he demanded it be *ventresca*, "from the belly," and the most tender if fished and not netted. With food culture, one becomes more demanding and also less apt to be deceived by the seller. I never considered questioning a fish salesman about how the fish was fished or what part of the fish I was purchasing.

While buying fillets of fish, Jean Claude questioned how the average person who is not an expert in fish could determine if the fillet to be purchased was what it was supposed to be. Since the French, like the Italians, Chinese, and other ethnic groups, are accustomed to seeing, buying, and eating fish whole, head to fin, they learn the  characters of the fish. They are more apt to distinguish and enjoy its unique flavor, detect and appreciate freshness and be reluctant to buy unless they know for sure what it is they are purchasing. This is another major difference in food culture.

From the fish hall, we went to the greatest display of meat products in the world. Walking through what seemed like miles of carcasses and customers bickering with vendors over prices, Jean Claude explained that by looking at the color of the meat, he could closely determine the diet of the animal.

When it came to buying the *foie gras* to make his *pâté de foie gras*, Jean Claude looked over at the duck livers displayed under a glass cover and started yelling at the salesman over the price. Jean Claude was so agitated that he suggested stopping for a drink. I had assumed he meant a coffee and croissant, but in fact he enjoyed an early morning glass of champagne while proclaiming, "This is not a day to buy *foie gras. Merde, merde!*" They were apparently out of the goose liver he wanted and the duck liver was not quite the right color. "The best is gone," he said.

Touring Rungis would never be the same as it was for me that day, being able to soak up the atmosphere with a professional French chef who knew all corners of the 250 hectares as if it was his own neighborhood. It reminded me that without true food culture, people are familiar only with most products after being sliced, ground, mixed and prepared in disguised shapes, preventing them from knowing what it is or where it came from. Acceptance of this allows one to become subject to inferior products, often mislabeled and flavored with unknown chemicals and additives for longer shelf life.

The hall of fowl came next. I recognized only a few varieties of the birds that lay in hundreds of open crates, feathers and all. Jean Claude wanted only the delicate Bresse chickens for his restaurant. After another heated debate with a vendor, he bought his fowl. I was definitely ready to move on.

The beautiful display of fruits and vegetables in the produce hall provided a welcome respite from the halls of dead animals. Here, the colorful seasonal products were a photographer's dream. We were about to depart when Jean Claude remembered Jeannine's request to buy flowers. This was a beautiful way to end an amazing day, in a room full of rainbows of fresh flowers of all sizes, shapes, and colors.

8

Convivio: A Financial Disaster

"The more of us value food, cheer and song above hordes of gold,
it will be a merrier world"

— JOHN TOLKIEN

My husband and I worked hard with limited resources to fulfill our version of the American dream. In over thirty years, we achieved a success far beyond our expectations. We had three successful restaurants, three amazing children, a beautiful waterfront home in Newport Beach, California, an active life in society, and many wonderful friends. Above all, we were blessed with good health and true happiness. We had the universe in our arms.

As an extremely successful plastic surgeon, my husband had made much of this possible. Our conservative European upbringing helped, too, leading us to have a comfortable home as our primary investment.

Our restaurants, catering business, social activities, medical meetings, and hospital events filled our days. When, out of the blue, our accountant suggested that I take over the 10,000-square-foot lease of a failing restaurant club, I laughed at the idea. I certainly didn't have time for another endeavor, especially not one so out of the realm of my experience. I favored family-run operations small enough to allow me to be hands-on and in control.

The accountant persisted, suggesting that I take on the project with the help of a managing partner, a client of his who supposedly had a wealth of experience in managing dinner-and-dance establishments. The accountant assured me that the location was excellent and that the lease would allow us to do whatever we wished without restrictions. I still had absolutely no interest.

A few weeks later, my husband and I flew to a medical meeting in Spain. The International Society of Plastic Surgeons puts on wonderful meetings, usually in exciting locations with amazing cultural, educational, and social activities. These meetings always included evenings of good food, music, and dancing, and I valued them as opportunities to meet and enjoy friends from around the world.

I returned to California after that meeting in Spain and left for work early in the morning. On the way, I passed joggers running along the highway and breathing dirty fumes from the heavy traffic. I couldn't help but compare these joggers with my friends in Spain from the night before. Dancing to the beat of the Gypsy Kings while enjoying music and *convivio* was a much more enjoyable exercise. A call from my accountant interrupted my thoughts of Spain, and at that moment, my DNA influenced me to make a decision that would change our family's lifestyle forever, as I had this impulsive thought: Why not bring my life in the piazzas of Europe to Newport Beach, as I had experienced in Europe.

My Italian DNA is at the center of my heart and soul. It is very useful at times, helping me make the best of lousy situations, face adversity, and embrace new experiences. This gusto for life can be at times irrational, too. Not long after that call, I signed a twenty-year lease on the advice of our business accountant, leaving the small print for him to decipher.

I designed an excellent restaurant concept and named it Ellis Island International Eatery. My plan was to feature different countries every week, along with their cuisines, music, dance, and culture. The concept everyone thought was excellent, except for competing businesses that had planned on my exit before I opened my doors. *The Daily Pilot*, our local paper, described my concept very well, saying that I was offering "a culinary festival of '*camaraderia*' with ethnic foods from around the world to play a greater role than drinking."

Our main room, Union Hall, was a food hall with four hundred small items from around the world on the menu. The room had a long bar with twenty beers on tap from around the world. We also offered an extensive international wine list. In the center of the room was a dance floor surrounded by informal communal wooden tables. I pictured our guests enjoying drinks and small dishes, as I had done in the tapas bars in Spain and across the *piazzas* in Europe, where bars and restaurants typically meet all social and economic needs, serving small dishes for a few dollars and providing a democratic meeting place for people of all ages and backgrounds to come together to enjoy foods and *convivio* rather than focus on drinking.

The back room, which I called the "Clubroom," had two upscale billiard tables, surrounded by smaller game tables, and there were three other rooms for more private dining. Each of these was decorated elegantly with fine china, silver cutlery, and crystal glasses. We would meet the needs of all age groups in the community, as well as their nutritional and economical needs. What the community did not offer I tried to do by way of putting our entire estate at risk.

In addition, we sold books and gift items in a small boutique, and the entrance featured our Ellis Island wall, where we posted pictures Orange County residents had sent us of ancestors who had entered the U.S. via Ellis Island. Ellis Island T-shirts became a very popular gift item, especially for the relatives of those who had immigrated to the U.S.

I imagined Ellis Island International Eatery as a convivial meeting place for all ages, like the piazzas of Europe. Before this, Newport Beach had no center where families and people of all ages could meet. To me, Ellis Island had a special meaning, too. It represented freedom and opportunity to immigrants from around the world just like my parents.

The nightmare began even before we opened our doors. I was surprised that this building in the city of Newport Beach, supposedly checked by both local health and building departments, had passed inspection. The interior had grimy floors, faulty appliances, filthy curtains, and crawling insects. The exterior had dangerous exposed electrical wires on the roof. I registered a complaint challenging the health department's previous inspections. My husband cautioned me, saying it could be detrimental to my other establishments. I was not concerned. Our What's Cooking Bistro was being completely remodeled and everything was new, including a wood-fired pizza oven.

To my surprise, my husband was right. Soon after we reopened our Bistro, the health department inspector came by and noted a violation with our new oven. It had a butcher block in front of it, so that my eighty-year-old mother, who made our bread, could cut it on the board. The inspector explained that someone could sneeze on the butcher block. This made no sense to me, since someone could sneeze on our table settings. The inspector asked me to remove the wooden cutting board without questioning her review of our operation and threatened to have our violation posted in the local paper.

I wondered afterward if I was being singled out. The next incident confirmed my suspicions.

By working diligently for months, we had managed to remove the trash and hanging wires from our new location and we had replaced bug-infested wooden beams. Rehabbing the space to meet city codes and regulations ate up most of our working capital, but I was committed to the lease and had to go forward with the project. While we were preparing for our opening, a local maître d' friend stopped by and said, "I feel sorry for you, doing all of this work. You're wasting your time and money." He went on to explain that there were plans in the works to close us down before we opened.

When I refused to believe him, he asked if I knew the police chief. "No," I said. "Never had a need to know him."

My friend advised me to meet with the chief, as he explained, you are no longer working in a deserted center at the end of the world. You are now competing with the big guys on the main drag. I didn't take him seriously, even when an employee confirmed that she had also heard of plans to close us down. Ellis Island International Eatery opened successfully despite the challenges. The customers loved us. However, our business neighbors seemed anxious to thwart our plans and began spreading vicious rumors, claiming I said things that were not true, determined to close us down before we opened. I responded from Italy with a fax

I had Jorge hand deliver to the family. My letter was never answered, which made me realize they may have been the source of the rumor. With a twenty-year lease and a personal guarantee, there was no way for me to get out of this commitment. I leveraged my restaurants and our home, and reopened in the same location with a new dance club concept.

Opening night at Lucy's Bayside Bar Grill exceeded anything Newport Beach had ever seen before. We were filled to capacity. Traffic was jammed and lines of people wrapped around the block. Two hours after opening, the fire department showed up to deal with the overcrowding. This happened every night of our first week. I finally walked right up to the battalion chief and said, "Why are you doing this to us?" He answered that he was just following the police chief's orders.

This obviously called for a meeting. I went to the police station with our three children, who were now young adults respected in the community. His secretary said the police chief wanted to see me alone, which seemed strange. I wanted him to meet our children, who were running the operation. My appointment was brief. With his hands caressing my arms, the chief told me that as long as I cooperated, there would be no problems. I never knew what he meant by "cooperate," but told my daughter when exiting the room that he gave me the creeps. Shortly after that, I was shocked to read news headlines about the police chief being fired due to accusations of rape and sexual discrimination. The press reported that the chief was connected to an almost mafia-type business group that controlled the city, and had the power to open and close any business for any reason. I was apparently one of their targets.

Despite the ongoing harassment and rumors, the crowds continued to come. Lucy's Bayside Club was a safe, clean, and fun place, and it filled a long-standing need in the community. A Western dance instructor wrote in our local newspaper that it was the cleanest and most organized club to which he'd ever brought a dancer. However, the relentless harassment continued for months, eventually forcing us to close our doors.

Unfortunately, the financial dominoes kept falling. My sons had taken over active management of the Bistro in the 1990s and continued dealing with the ongoing issues. The Irvine Company wanted more income from us. With so little seating and a packed house, there wasn't much more we could do with the existing space to increase revenue. We rented the adjoining space, paying a considerable amount of money for renovations.

Once completed, the pressure continued when the company wanted us to remodel the outdoor seating area. Nothing we did earned their satisfaction. Unbeknownst to our family, while encouraging us to expand the restaurant capacity inside and out, the Irvine Company was quietly making plans to evict us. They were just waiting for the right opportunity. The area had developed after some 25 years, now catering to a high-income clientele, and was moving on to becoming one of the most successful counties in California.

My sons gave them that opportunity when they questioned the high cost of cleaning our grease trap. Per our lease agreement, we were required to maintain the trap, and I had faithfully paid to have that done professionally for decades. Jorge and Jason investigated further and determined that the grease trap was not just ours, but serviced the entire shopping center! When they complained to property management, they were told it was still their responsibility, according to the lease. When they threatened to inform the health department, the relationship with management quickly deteriorated.

Eventually, the management team resolved the issue, but it involved digging into the floor of our kitchen. We temporarily closed the Bistro and lost income, pinching our cash flow. This led to us having to pay our rent a little late. The Irvine Company, which feared we would leave the deserted center and previously had been tolerant of late rent payments, was suddenly playing by new rules. Management informed us that rent was to be paid on time, regardless of the circumstances. This was another devastating blow not only to our pride, but also to our financial situation, and we had to close the Bistro's doors, unable to fight the big guys who, we have been told, waited for this opportunity to kick us out since they knew that the community wanted us to remain. Many suggested that we petition as others had done and, I understand, won, and are still in their locations today, but unfortunately we did not.

We were incredulous as we watched the Irvine Company spend money on maintaining and promoting the property after we left, putting in comfortable lounge chairs, tables, flower pots and creating the beautiful setting I requested for 28 years. We had waited almost three decades for something like this. In a front-page article in the local paper, the company reported that we had failed to pay our rent, and stated that they regretted the fact that we had to leave. I wrote an angry response letter. They printed my letter, which more accurately described the

---

Tues- Sept 2, 2003

Irvine Co. serving up misinformation

By Lucy Ann Luhan

To clarify some misunderstandings due to an article in the July 24 Daily Pilot, I would like to state that I am still the administrator of a bed and breakfast and cooking school in Tuscany, Italy. The article, "Soon, the answer will be tacos," said I had been running it until recently. I also continue to operate our restaurant, Luciana's in Dana Point, and What's Cooking Catering Service.

Having received numerous calls condemning the Irvine Co. for their statements made to the press regarding What's Cooking Bistro, I felt it best to ignore the issue. But, when the Irvine Co. attempted to defend itself, as a company official did in a July 30 letter to the editor from the Irvine Co.'s president of retail development, Keith Eyrich, "A painful end to a long relationship with What's Cooking," I felt a response to his statements is warranted.

• "Painful End." If so painful, why did they kick us out after we took out a loan to remodel, with three more years on our lease?

Concerning the termination of the lease, we were told what statements will be made to the public, "Luhan family will focus their attention on another restaurant." That is not the reason for our departure. Following the Daily Pilot article, we received a notice from the Irvine Co.'s attorney that stated, "your client has made a series of statements to the media that clearly violate the express terms of the termination agreement. . . . We certainly hope that this actionable conduct by your client does not persist." Are they ashamed of their conduct, or does the Irvine Co. have something to hide?

• "A difficult decision designed to help the Luhans out of a difficult financial situation." I, the guarantor of the lease, had never been contacted by the Irvine Co. nor were our finances discussed. The Irvine Co. decided to inform the press to make the company look innocent, not considering the detrimental effect their statements would have on our other businesses, employees and purveyors.

"When informed by our attorney that the Irvine Co. wanted us to leave the center, they were asked if they had another tenant. They answered, "no." Unfortunately for the Irvine Co. we knew the future tenant who was considering the location, whom I understand was forbidden to tell us of the company's plan.

Proof of the Irvine Co.'s mishandling of our situation can be viewed in the front page of the Daily Pilot article, in a statement made by Jennifer Heiger, Irvine Co. spokeswoman, that we were six months behind in rent. I resent very much this defamation of our family. Does one really believe that the Irvine Co. would allow six months? Then Eyrich wrote in his letter to the editor that we were three months behind, in the back pages of the paper. There seems to be no shame in defaming a family if it makes the company look good.

• "Their success is our success." Do they really believe the public would believe this? All the calls I have received prove differently.

The time finally arrived that the center was attractive and the area developed; this could have been the best opportunity in 28 years to truly become successful. Never did I realize until this occurred how many tenants experience this situation, but nobody bothers to tell their story. I would not either, until I read Eyrich's letter on how they did this to help us "avoid further losses." If sincere, they could reimburse us for the loan we had to get to remodel the Bistro, knowing we had a five-year extension [on the lease]. That would help avoid further losses more than words.

Having experienced drain problems throughout the years, we have always corrected the problem as required in our lease, at our expense. Recently the stench became so horrendous, sending customers out of our restaurant, that an examination by a plumbing firm was called. The management firm of the Irvine Co. was reluctant to come to assist, since the problem was always handled by us.

It was only when we threatened management that we would report them to the county health department because of the raw sewerage floating in the grease trap that they decided to correct the problem.

This created a deep trench in the middle of our kitchen. Our staff had to step over and view the four-foot-high pile of dirt, consisting of raw sewerage, human waste and toilet tissue. We had no choice but to close our operations. When asked to be reimbursed for our closure, we were denied. At this point the Bistro threatened the Irvine Co.'s management company, for the first time, with a lawsuit. Could this be the reason that we were not given a chance to stay?

We would like to thank our friends, customers, and the wonderful neighborhood that has supported us through the 28 years in this center and to thank all those who have called us expressing their sorrow in seeing us leave. Special thanks to Mayor Bromberg and the City Council, who presented our family with a proclamation last month, honoring the Luhan family. He expressed the council's regret of our departure and how the closing of What's Cooking Bistro will be a loss to the community. Newport's first family Bistro.

In conclusion, there appears to be a contradiction as to the cause of our departure. According to our attorney, a statement made by the Irvine Co. to him was, "We don't want them in the center anymore," yet that is not to be publicized. What they are asking us to sign is that even though we are being kicked out, we must tell the public we wanted to be kicked out. I see no need to make this inaccurate statement to our community.

Certainly we will concentrate on our location in Dana Point — Luciana's Ristorante — but that is not the reason for our departure.

• EDITOR'S NOTE: Lucy Ann Luhan was the owner of What's Cooking Bistro, which closed in July.

76

reasons for our departure. In retrospect, instead of the letter, I should have sought legal counsel.

Later, the Irvine Company issued corrections, printed on an obscure back page of the paper. Our mailbox was flooded with letters of support and many of our customers begged us to fight back. This meant the world to us and helped preserve our family's reputation in the community. However, we lacked the funds to battle such a big corporation.

Apparently, the Irvine Company failed to see the value of our community connections. They failed to see what others, including the restaurant reviewer for *Zagat*, who described our family as people who were "motivated by the joy of cooking rather than the ringing of the cash register," saw.

Thankfully, others in the area were more appreciative of our time in Newport Beach. The Newport Harbor Chamber of Commerce issued a proclamation, saying that our family had "set the standards for Orange County's ever evolving culinary landscape." The Chamber of Commerce issued a proclamation to the Luhan family, which was televised, saying that we had "set the standards for Orange County's ever evolving culinary landscape through their family-owned and operated neighborhood bistro, the first bistro in Orange County." It was also noted that the Luhan family had been actively involved in the Newport Beach community for decades and Lucy Luhan "a well-known philanthropist, after 28 years in business, is sadly closing the bistro doors."

Mayor Steven Bloomberg congratulated the Luhan family for "their many years of servicing the public" and added, "They will be sorely missed." Again, following this Chamber meeting, we received thousands of letters of support from the community. On our last night, friends packed the Bistro and the center; Mom and my sisters came to give me support.

Those years in the shopping center have rewarded me and my family with so many wonderful friends, many of whom have followed us to Italy. I have a treasure chest of memories that hoards of gold money could not buy. What is seen in popular Italian films, generations of people talking, gesturing and laughing, while passionately passing platters of different foods, drinking wine and enjoying the moment, is in fact our life in Italy today with Orange County friends and their friends. Many have learned the meaning of *convivio* and the art of living the simple pleasures. As Marcella Hazan, the late reigning *doyenn* of Italian cooking in America, stated, "Eating in Italy is one more manifestation of the Italians' age-old gift of making an art out of life."

Closing our establishments resulted in a collapse of my universe, setting off a financially devastating chain of events that ultimately resulted in the loss of our home. My only option was to go to the once abandoned farmhouse in Italy to enjoy *convivio* where I first was introduced to it, in a society that understands the happiness and health benefits *convivio* can give an individual, a family, and a nation. I firmly believe many social problems related to the dissolution of the family could be brought to rest with a return of enjoying the simple pleasures of the table with family and friends, whenever possible leaving no one to eat alone.

My father often quoted Giuseppe Verdi, saying, "You may have the universe, as long as I have Italy." I prayed and hoped that Verdi and my father were right. For we had no choice. We left our waterfront home in California for a farm with a broken roof in Tuscany.

Life in Tuscany

"The best sauce you can give your guests is a happy expression on your face
and heartfelt hospitality."

—Artusi

When I made that impulsive deposit on the Tuscan farm, I had imagined it would be our family's vacation home, not our permanent address. Nonetheless, with a lot of hard work, the abandoned farmhouse became our home. Villa Lucia also became a beloved retreat for many friends, and for people who started out as strangers but often become our friends as well.

Beautiful letters continue to reward me with wonderful memories with wonderful new friends.

By Marcus Ray

On the train from Florence to Montecattini, You and I

Take an excursion to the country through the Tuscan hills,

Passing verdant gardens and small towns with their golden

Colored buildings with red tiled roofs, arriving in the

Caring arms of Villa Lucia, amidst the delightful olive

Groves and resplendent landscape of welcome we receive

From the lady of the house, so hospitable and loving to her guests.

Peace and quiet abound, and the view overlooking the valley

Is the essence of an Italian mood, glimpsed through

The gray green foliage of the olive trees, just below

The coziness of the portico off the kitchen, stretching

Its sublime atmosphere into the distance, drifting miles

Away toward the silhouette of the blue gray mountains

That forms the edge of the great valley's bowl.

High above the overture of this valley view,

Villa Lucia provides our haven into another world

Of heaven on earth. The lady of the Villa, with her

Tender loving care, restored this 500 year old farmhouse

Into a place of total beauty and warm welcome. She cares

For her guests like fine china, or royal charges, and shares

Of herself in a most generous way. We are blessed

By our stay here. Relaxation reaches new heights in the

Blessings of true hospitality. The Tuscan air fills our lungs

Afresh, and the stillness of nature envelopes us, and

Elevates our souls to partake of a worldly paradise.

In the Kitchen of Villa Lucia

In the kitchen of your pure hospitality I am made whole,

Accepting the motherly love you give to all of your guests

In the food and drink of a Tuscan country grace.

The kitchen is my favorite room in the Villa of Lucia's

Outpouring joy. She is so happy to serve and converse,

To remove the tired concerns of her people from afar,

Removing their small fears of being on foreign soil,

So glad to give her stories in the tongue of her

Countrymen.

Here, amidst the fertile crops of Tuscan soil,

She has risen to the heights of her greatest gifts:

To give to her guests from the heart of her Love

To serve people, to feed people, to put a well

Appointed roof over their heads.

I love Lucia's kitchen. The massive wood beam

Forms the lintel above the stove, the large silver range

Sits ready to cook the meal; the solid marble sink

Is so firm in its naturally sculpted presence.

And the table supports the circle of dining and talking

That completes the cycle of Italian social life.

I am grateful to be in the embrace of Villa Lucia.

It is a place beyond the calculations of the hotel

Industry; the thick walls of "business" do not exist here.

I rather feel at home and able to rest, with permission

To help myself to a snack, in the pastoral environment

Of natural beauty, in the kitchen of Divine Providence

That is the heart of Lucia's Villa!

The Bed & Breakfast/cooking school concept was inspired by some of our restaurant customers from California, who sought us out to see what we were doing in Italy. They loved the cultural experience and some even requested cooking classes. Before long, groups interested in cooking classes and Italian culture started reserving weeks on the calendar. Our California customers brought their friends, and our B&B was officially in business. The venue had changed from California to Italy, but I was still in the service industry, following my passion to create *convivio*.

At our farmhouse in Tuscany, we make every effort to demonstrate the importance not only of good food, but of *convivio*. Our life on the farm centers on the table, and we introduce friends and new guests to that lifestyle through cooking classes, harvesting products from our organic garden, and sampling our certified extra virgin olive oil. I have surmised from their thank-you notes that, for many of our guests, their new experiences with us in Tuscany gave them something more important than good food: unforgettable memories of *convivio*. Our guests have commented that time at the table here is "magical."

Many of our guests return home feeling inspired to incorporate this special family time into their lives there. As one guest wrote, "Only by experiencing food culture that is observed in all aspects of daily life in Italy can one learn to understand and appreciate the merits of genuine food and *convivio*."

One event that left a lasting impression on me during my first years in Tuscany was when all of the neighbors came to help me harvest our wine grapes. When I asked my neighbor, Franco, what I could do to reciprocate, he told me that on the farm, neighbors help neighbors without any expectation of material reward. Knowing that I wouldn't have the time to help all of them with their harvests, I asked him what could I do? He suggested inviting them over for dinner.

That evening, listening to the laughter, the singing, and the guitar player strumming the famous Neapolitan songs of yesterday, I experienced one of the best examples of community living. This confirmed what I had observed previously in small villages. People tend to be more social, more dependent on one another, and therefore more appreciative of one another. Chores never seem to be as much work when neighbors gather to work together. Daily tasks become simple pleasures.

As I enjoyed chatting with my Tuscan neighbors, I couldn't help but think about how I had once been in a California *gelateria* when I ran into my financial advisor. We chatted about the economy while enjoying our gelato.

A month later, my husband asked me about a service charge on the accountant's invoice. I had no idea that our conversation was "on the clock!" Meanwhile, our Italian farm neighbors helped each other without monetary rewards. Like me, they had been taught that giving time and attention to others enhances your life more than material rewards.

In addition to leading me to form friendships with generous neighbors and our B&B guests, my life in Tuscany helped me heal after our financial disaster in California because of the valuable lessons I learned from local artisans. I try to bring our B&B guests to see these craftspeople whenever possible.

One of our favorite stops is with Giovanni, known to his friends as Nino, the last of more than one hundred copper artisans who lived in the Pescia area of Tuscany. At ninety-two years old, he still hammers away every day to craft wonderful cooking pots and sees no reason to retire.

I have always treasured the copper pots lining my kitchen walls. I have been collecting them for some forty years, and I love them even more now, knowing the time and craftsmanship that has gone into making each one. During our frequent conversations, Nino often discusses how the amazing culinary skills of the Italians originated with lives of poverty that demanded culinary creativity if they were going to survive. "All foods were considered gifts of survival," he says.

During Nino's youth, for instance, refined white flour wasn't available. Bread was made from whatever was available, including linseed, acorns, or vine roots. Bread was never discarded, because even stale bread could be creatively repurposed. Bread-based recipes have been passed down through generations. *Panzanella* uses stale bread, vegetables, herbs, and olive oil in a great summer salad dish. Soups such as *pappa di pomodoro*. made with stale bread, tomatoes, olive oil, and fresh basil, were once survival dishes that, according to Nino, originated during *La Miseria,* the most difficult epoch of Italian history.

Today, when served a popular appetizer known as *bruschetta*, Nino remembers how, in years past, stale bread topped with onions or rubbed with garlic was often all that was available for dinner. Fresh herbs were substituted for salt, a luxury at the time. Garden fresh hot peppers were used to preserve foods; food was often grilled with wood to enhance flavors.

In spite of the fact that more resources are available, the traditional Italian diet refuses to follow changing trends. It is a simple diet born of hunger in the past, and it has become one of the healthiest and economical ways of eating. Leftover vegetables, beans, pasta, or even just a potato or two would become a delicious dinner *frittata* by adding some eggs, something my mother often did. At the restaurant, I made a simple *frittata* by adding an egg or two to unsold fresh vegetables, and the customers raved about my "gourmet quiche."

The traditional Italian homemaker can make a pasta meal with little more than a chicken or a quail egg and a cup of flour. In a pinch, adding water to the flour worked, too. With basic kitchen ingredients such as olive oil, hot pepper, and garlic, she could make a pasta sauce and feed her family a delicious, wholesome, economical meal.

Never had I imagined that walking through the warped green double doors of Nino's aging *bottega* would influence my life so much. "What more does one need in life?" he would often remind me, reflecting on life's two most basic needs: food for fueling our physical bodies, and love to fuel our hearts and souls. Sharing his philosophy of living and his appreciation of life's simple pleasures made me reflect on my own life and helped me move on from the financial disasters that had plagued us in California.

Today, there are industrial machines that can quickly hammer out copper cooking and baking pieces, but Nino remains passionate about artisanal wares. He takes pleasure in showing my guests and me how a flexible, soft, raw copper sheet is strengthened by hammering. One day, noticing me glance at the piles of copper scraps on the floor of his work area, he smiled and said, "These pieces of copper may have had their origin years ago," and explained that a hundred percent of the copper he uses is recycled. All his handmade items can be purchased in his bottega. My husband and I surprised Nino with a birthday cake.

Watching Nino bang away at sheets of copper and use his skills to transform it into a small frying pan, I would listen to his many stories of *"La Miseria,"* days when the Italians suffered famine, invaders and war. He repeated often, *"La Miseria* is the best teacher." He confirmed what my parents had told me from their personal experiences, saying how, during World War II, the German soldiers took over many of the Italian farmhouses. More important than the locations were the farm products, like the canned vegetables from summer gardens and homemade preserves from

basements that Italian farm families had prepared and stored to withstand famine or harsh winters. Soldiers quickly realized that the diet of the farmers may have been meager, but the food was often much better than that of the city dwellers, many of whom starved to death due to their inability to obtain food.

From 1940 to 1946, when Italy experienced its worst rationing period, the most basic ingredients became the culture of the hungry. My parents had already moved to America by that time, but Nino explained how even *lumache* (snails) were a blessing to

find, because with a little bread, they became a meal for the family. Desperate people would go out at night to search for these slimy creatures by moonlight. Little birds were often hunted and killed, too, and might be a family's only source of meat. Wild greens and weeds picked in the fields were eaten raw or served in watered-down soup.

Even today, frugal Italians who appreciate the nutritional benefits of fresh produce search the fields searching for edible wild greens. In our Tuscan fields, just before it is time to plow, strangers come and pick what I used to consider nothing more than weeds. They leave a bag of freshly picked wild greens at our front door, sharing the fruits of their labor.

Our olive oil class attendees visited Nino after pressing olives one day and I presented him with a bottle of our fresh olive oil. He thanked me and explained how the olive itself was a staple during hard times. For centuries, farmers sold their best olives, made olive oil with the second best, and put the rest on their bread. Olive oil in times past was really a survival food. Today, kitchens around the world use it to create and flavor wonderful meals. *Bruschetta* with olive oil, once simple survival food, has become popular around the globe.

Nino has shared countless such stories about his experiences with poverty, which I believe contributed to his excellent character. The peasant farmers had to learn how to preserve foods to survive the winter when the garden would no longer produce. They created ways to preserve summer vegetables by placing them in jars, covering them in olive oil, and storing them in cellars for consumption during the winter or to sell to people living in the city. This tradition continues today among many Italians. In homes with three generations living together, this kind of frugality is still common. Many of these foods have become specialty items in gourmet restaurants and markets, commanding high prices. In Italy today, as in the past, everyone eats what the rural farmers do, seeking genuine quality products. There continues to be little distinction between classes or economic conditions when it comes to food.

Poverty in Italy led to incredible uses for things that otherwise might have been seen as a waste. After getting every drop of juice from grapes to make wine, who but a peasant farmer would think of using the stems and seeds to make the Italian liqueur *grappa*?

Italians took the flavored ice treat from the Arabs and perfected the art of chilling it to make some of the best gelatos in the world. After making sorbet with fresh lemon juice, they found a way to use the lemon rinds to make limoncello, the popular after-dinner drink. The humble tomato, initially thought to be poisonous when brought to Europe from South America, was made into tomato sauce for pasta dishes and pizza.

I often returned home after visiting Nino thinking about how wonderful it is to know a person filled with so much purpose. His way of life is so simple, yet clearly brings him joy. It is unfortunate that today, with greater economic comforts, there are fewer master artisans who can offer the life lessons we all need about the importance of taking responsibility for our actions, living harmoniously with others, and being happy with what we have.

In one of our cooking classes at the B&B, I asked the attendees to make a dinner from whatever was available in my pantry. Seeing their perplexed faces made me realize that they were lost without recipes. They probably did not have a mother in the kitchen showing them practical and simple ways to feed a family with a few quality foods.

When no suggestions came forward, I demonstrated how a simple can of tuna can be sautéed with some fresh parsley, hot pepper, and good olive oil and served over pasta for a quick dinner for four. Many of our family's pasta sauces are made as the pasta is being cooked. Sauces can be created from endless combinations of basic ingredients found in most kitchens. Any leftover vegetables, meat, or fish can be served over pasta. No pasta? Serve it over rice. No rice? Serve it over eggs. There is no need to always rely on recipes. It takes just a few minutes and a little imagination to make a meal with a handful of simple ingredients. One of the attendees asked what I could make with a can of tomato sauce, other than pasta sauce. I cut up a big onion and a green pepper and began sautéing them, then added a jar of our homegrown pureed

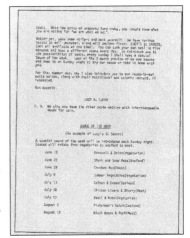

tomatoes. After ten minutes, I slid four eggs into the tasty tomato sauce. In minutes, I had dinner for two.

A *scamorza* cheese is a firm, dry mozzarella made with cow's milk and tied with a string on the upper third to create a pear-shaped cheese. When I asked if anyone had any ideas for this type of mozzarella, I was again amazed that the only suggestion was to use it in a *Caprese* salad. I described various ways of using mozzarella, from omelets in the morning to a quick dinner that required nothing more than cooking the cheese for a minute on each side, slicing some good crusty bread, and serving it with a salad.

Our class also discussed cooking one day a week and freezing food as a solution for busy homemakers. Some felt this defeats the purpose of home cooking, especially when meals, as demonstrated that day, can be made so quickly and easily with fresh ingredients. Some in the class disagreed, preferring to keep something on hand in the freezer. I partially agreed, explaining that I do love to have some good stock around, but I freeze it in paper cups so that I can just tear off the cup and use the desired amount. You can make a meal in minutes by adding anything you have available to the stock: vegetables (fresh, frozen, canned, or leftover), beans, fish, meat, or pasta, just to name a few. Eggs can be quickly beaten up with some good *parmigiano* cheese and fresh parsley added for one of my favorite evening soups, *stracciatella*. Toast a few slices of country bread with good olive oil, and "*ecco*," dinner is ready.

Most Italians are reluctant to buy frozen products or freeze dinners in advance. When shopping in large markets in Italy, there are always lines to buy fresh fish, meat, cheeses, or cold cuts, and every shopping trip is a delight.

One day, I was shopping at the outdoor food market with an American friend, a student studying art and Italian in Florence, when I notice her standing mesmerized at a cheese vendor's stand. She watched as the cheese vendor described the farm where the milk came from to a shopper and produced the wheel of *caciotta* that he was about to slice for her to sample. He suggested buying this particular *caciotta* because it was the best one for her young child, being made with eighty percent cow's milk and twenty percent sheep's milk, unlike the one she was about to purchase, which was made only with cow's milk. He reasoned that it was tastier and had a smaller percentage of fat. The woman smiled as she admitted that she loved fatty cheeses, particularly the dense fontina, even though she knew it was forty-five percent fat.

As Julie waited patiently to buy some *pecorino*, a customer with a northern accent interrupted their conversation by volunteering a recipe for the *fontina*. By the time the vendor was ready to serve Julie, she realized she had just been given a mini "Cheese Making 101" course.

Practicing her Italian, Julie was finally able to ask the vendor for some pecorino. When he asked, "What kind?" she turned to me for help. Before I could answer her question, a discussion broke out among the customers standing nearby, who all had their favorite cheese and reasons why they liked it best, most often because it was from their hometown.

Next, the vendor asked Julie what she wanted to do with her cheese. She looked over at me and said all she wanted was to replicate what I had served that morning. I explained that for breakfast, I usually served a young, soft pecorino from Siena, but after dinner, I preferred an aged pecorino from Sardegna. Walking away after purchasing one hundred grams of fresh pecorino, Julie looked at me and said, "Do you realize we have been at this cheese stand for twenty minutes?"

Welcome to Italy, I thought, where people love to talk about food almost as much as they love to eat it.

My favorite cheese vendor at our farmer's market offers samples of *parmigiano reggiano,* which I consider the king of cheeses. He starts with a young one-year-old  and ends with a sharp, dry, strong, five-year-old *parmigiano*. His cheese display lists the different ages so shoppers know what they are buying. Most of our B&B attendees say they never knew there was such a difference when buying *parmigiana* in the United States.

When we approached the *prosciutto* vendor, I told Julie that she needed to be clear about what she intended to do with it, so he could help her accordingly. Was it for a sandwich, to complement an oven dish, to wrap around asparagus, to put in a *frittata*, or to serve with summer melon? Did she prefer salty, moderately salty, sweet or aged, and from what region? San Daniele, made in the Friuli-Venezia region, tends to be dark and sweet and many people favor this type. As for a slice to complement sweet melon, many would prefer the sweet and slightly salty *prosciutto* from Parma.

Various regions of Italy produce *prosciutto*, I explained, but the city of Parma claims to be the best and is the most popular around the world. Many believe the sea breeze from the Versilia region is one of the keys for making this type of prosciutto, as well as the unique preparation and curing process. *Parmigiano reggiano* is made in this area and the whey (liquid part) left over from making the *parmigiana* is used to make ricotta. The remaining liquid from the ricotta-making process is added to the feed of the local pigs. This, the people of Parma believe, is the reason for the delicate taste of their local *prosciutto*. In addition, as is true for most *prosciuttos*, its fat content is low, it has no carbohydrates, it is a raw food item, it travels well, and it's easy to digest.

At this point, Julie decided to skip her language classes later in the week so that she could go with our cooking group to Parma to see the production process and learn more about these artisan-made products.

Many of our American guests had their first exposure to Italian food culture through our B&B and cooking school. Initially, they were surprised by our *pranzos*, which could last two hours or more at Villa Lucia, but they quickly learned to love and look forward to them. Many said they missed them when they were back in the United States. For many, time at the table was a new experience, and they tried to adopt *convivio* when they return home.

During my conversation with Julia Child at a food convention in San Diego in the 1980s, she had a clear message: "What is dangerous and discouraging about this era is that people really are afraid of food, and sitting down to dinner is a trap, not something to enjoy." Italians, on the other hand, believe that a relaxed setting helps us enjoy and digest our food better, allowing us to absorb more nutrients.

Many other countries with food culture recognize this as well. My Norwegian friends have a saying that "food and joy equal health." In Vietnam, food plays such a significant role that people are urged to "enjoy food that is delicious and served with affection for better health." Virginia Woolf also recognized the importance of food. She stated, "One can't think well, love well, sleep well, if one doesn't eat well."

Irwin Rosenberg, former dean of the Friedman School of Nutrition Science and Policy at Tufts University, said that when he and his committee tried to establish U.S. dietary guidelines, they found it difficult to make a statement encouraging eating a variety of foods because of the negative ideas many had toward eating. Today, researchers are confirming what Italians believe: Eating with people you enjoy is a means to better digestion—and better overall health.

Once we were living in Tuscany, my husband and I enjoyed attending various food fairs. One that particularly caught my attention was a chocolate and wine convention held in Perugia, a city in Umbria known for its dynasty of chocolatiers. We hoped that this event would give us not only the opportunity to experience one of the most beautiful, idyllic, and inspirational medieval hamlets in Italy, but to also enjoy two products we love: chocolate and wine.

The convention began with a morning chocolate tasting. There were rows of long tables with seating for twelve at each one. Each chair faced baskets of small, colorfully wrapped items in various shapes. While the lecturer began speaking, explaining how certain chocolates are best paired with different liquors, fruity wines, or after-dinner drinks, I began my journey into chocolate heaven.

About an hour into this decadent experience, the speaker suggested another particular violet-wrapped chocolate would be ideal with an after-dinner *grappa*. I turned to Jorge and explained that I had reached my limit and couldn't consume anymore.

"Good grief, Lucy!" Jorge said. "You're supposed to spit the chocolate into the spitting pot. Are you eating them all?"

Only then did I notice that the other participants had allowed the chocolates to last a few seconds in their mouths before spitting them out into stainless steel receptacles next to each basket. In my eagerness to taste the chocolates, I had paid no attention to the others, or to my bucket.

When we returned to our room, the huge basket of *Baci* (chocolate kisses) provided to guests by the hotel wasn't at all tempting. In fact, I covered it with a bath towel and placed it in the closet. I feared that I might wander in the night like a truffle dog digging for treasure.

On the second day, I decided to skip the beginning of the tasting and leave the others in the tasting hall. It was an effort to quell the uneasy feeling in my stomach that could worsen upon seeing or smelling more chocolate. I chose to wander about the hotel, only to discover more tempting chocolates to sample everywhere. At any other time, I would have loved to indulge in the free samples, but my stomach sent messages to cancel any temptations.

I did join the others for the closing speech. We were all delighted when the speaker announced that the gold medal winner of the 1994 International Convention of Chocolatiers in Paris was Slitti of Monsummano Terme, a place in our neighborhood where we often went for our morning coffee. We had no idea that the chocolates in Slitti's café display were made on the premises in a sterile kitchen downstairs from the coffee shop.

The contest had required entrants to produce an antique-looking object using only chocolate, and Slitti's entry was a replica of an antique clock. Made with dark, light, and white chocolate, the clock might easily have been mistaken for a treasure of yesterday, made of shiny mahogany wood with columns of ecru porcelain.

We had developed a wonderful friendship with the gracious Slitti family. One time, an invitation to dinner came with a two-foot-tall chocolate egg. On another occasion, we received a chocolate replica of an espresso coffee machine as a gift. The only problem with these beautiful Slitti-designed chocolates is that it's painful to break the amazing chocolate creations in order to taste and enjoy them.

Visiting the immaculate chocolate factory in the basement of the Slitti Café and watching the production process became a highlight for many of our Villa Lucia cooking class attendees. Andrea would patiently demonstrate the process of chocolate making and share the secrets to making some of his specialties, such as the chocolate spoons displayed in his shop upstairs. Later, it was no longer feasible for our groups to enjoy private lessons in the basement factory, as Slitti chocolate continued to win numerous awards, including the gold medal at the prestigious Olympics of Chocolate in Berlin.

I was surprised one hot summer day to see that the Slitti display case was nearly empty. When I asked why, Andrea told me that it was August. I mentioned that I could buy chocolates in the United States all year round. He went to the kitchen and came back with a piece of chocolate, which he put in the palm of my hand. Within seconds, my hand was covered with melted chocolate as he explained how chocolates sold in the U.S. usually had wax added to prevent them from melting, but he preferred to keep his pure. Pure dark chocolate was used centuries ago as an energy drink and aphrodisiac. In the early nineteenth century, he explained, chocolate became popular and was manufactured using additives to give it a longer shelf life.

The addition of sugars, milk, soy lecithin and paraffin resulted in an inferior product shunned by chocolatiers. The best chocolate makers demand that the only fats added to their chocolates be from the beans themselves, and artisan chocolatiers passionately continue to guard this traditional method of making them, despite the more time-consuming and labor-intensive production.

Luciano Slitti, Andrea's father, was a prominent coffee bean roaster and maker of custom coffee blends served at his café. While Andrea handled the chocolate business, his brother Daniele learned the coffee business from his father, where he perfected the art of roasting coffee beans.

Daniele shared his knowledge with our B&B cooking students, telling us that the two most popular kinds of beans are Arabica and Robusta. A good coffee bean roaster must take into consideration where the bean comes from: the plant's soil, the climate, the altitude, the characteristics  of the plant, as well as the harvest and processing methods. Every aspect affects the bean quality.

Before roasting, coffee beans have little inherent flavor. The beans begin their journey to coffee making when they absorb heat, giving off excess water in the form of steam as the dull green color of the beans begins to gain a yellowish tone. There are many varieties of raw coffee beans to select from, but it takes a skilled roaster to determine the aroma, taste, body, and roast of the finished product.

Our favorite coffee barman, Umberto Galligani, maintained his reputation as "King of Cappuccinos" until his death in 2015. For fifteen years, our one full-time employee, the maintenance manager, went to Umberto's coffee bar every morning, passing at least twenty other locations along the way. Soon, we were taking our Villa Lucia guests there, too.

Umberto started his training at age twelve and continued to make his special coffee for over seventy-three years. The crowds that came daily for their special coffee or cappuccino never allowed him to retire. He topped his coffees with designs made of cocoa powder—hearts for women and a certain male body part for men, which brought smiles every time. Umberto walked the room wearing a big smile and greeting everyone while adding extra warm or cold milk to those who needed an extra shot. When he passed away in 2015, the papers of Valdinievole reported that he was not a barman, but a

legendary artist who played an active part in the community.

I couldn't agree more. A good Italian barman like Umberto considers gauge pressure, water temperature, water quality, ground coffee quantity, duration of extraction, and volume of the liquid product when making a coffee. The pressure and temperature must be kept absolutely consistent with each shot of coffee and the water must be pure. The brewing ratio of coffee to water determines the strength of the coffee, not the darkness of the roast, as many people falsely assume. Most Italians like a strong coffee, but that doesn't mean a bitter coffee. Overexposure of the coffee grounds causes bitterness and under-extraction results in sourness. Italian espresso must be served hot and fresh before the highly volatile aromas dissipate.

In our California bistro, we had an imported Italian machine and a trained Italian coffee server. We used coffee imported from Italy, trying to emulate the Italian coffee experience as closely as possible for our guests, but for those who understood good coffee, mainly our Italian customers, it wasn't the same. I could not figure out why. This disparity became clear when a new Italian waiter joined us and said that we considered everything except an important ingredient, the water. We had never considered the water, yet that's one of the most important ingredients for a good cup of expresso. Shortly afterward, we received a notice from the city saying not to be concerned with the taste of chemicals in the water. It was safe to drink, but they said not to put it in fish bowls or give it to small animals! This was yet more evidence that you can only determine inferior food products by experiencing quality, assuming one has food culture.

The Taccini family of Vinci, well known in Tuscany, has been making ceramics for the last five hundred years. They have created major works of art which been sold worldwide. Shortly after I arrived in Tuscany in 1985, I met the four Taccini brothers and their father. Our friendship through the years brought them a number of times to our home in California. This included a special trip to assemble a large ceramic wall panel depicting medieval musicians called "Happy Harlequins." This massive, colorful masterpiece is over ten feet wide and almost four feet tall.

Alessandro Taccini, who specializes in clay artwork, brought the individual panels from Italy, then assembled the five pieces into one major panel to hang on the wall of our restaurant. It is their only major work of this size in the United States.

Alessandro has been making ceramic objects out of Tuscan clay since age twelve. His brothers do the painting and kiln firing. I loved visiting their *bottega* and seeing my exuberant friends, who have a true passion for their craft. Alessandro's hospitality and generosity are always appreciated by our B&B guests and friends, too, as he deftly demonstrates how he makes various objects.

He even allows many of our guests to try making pieces of art, and is always happy to offer suggestions to novice artists. Alessandro and his brothers speak openly of the passion they feel for the work they do, and of their regret that their craft is dying. Their children, for the first time in the family's five-hundred-year history, will not continue in their footsteps.

Besides his talent as a ceramist, Alessandro is a great pizza-maker. We have a big wood-burning pizza oven in our home, and on the last night of their cooking classes, we often offer our guests an evening of music and pizza. Alessandro also invites our guests to join his family for *convivio*

at his *bottega* for a taste of old Tuscan cuisine. He and his lovely wife, Juliana, always prepare traditional Tuscan dishes for our guests and explain, as Nino does, that their dishes originated in times of famine and poverty. The guests are always amazed by how tasty and satisfying these peasant dishes can be.

My children thought it was strange when I brought a pasta machine as a housewarming gift to a chef in France in 1981 at the start of the pasta craze. But they were even more surprised by the hostess gifts I received from European guests.

When our French friends visited us in Tuscany for the first time, Jean Claude walked into our kitchen, hands behind his back, and announced that he was bringing me a beautiful and lasting bouquet. The *ail rose de Lautrec* is a bouquet that has certainly lasted longer than any other bouquet of flowers I had ever received. The fragrant pink garlic bulbs are a gastronomic emblem from the Lautrec area of France, and this tightly-wound bundle accented many of my Tuscan dishes for the months it decorated my kitchen in Villa Lucia.

On his next visit, Jean Claude presented me with a box of quail and blackbirds that he had hunted that morning in the French countryside before driving to our farmhouse. Beautifully dressed in their black and gray feathers, they were lying side by side in their wooden crate and presented a sad sight. Jorge worked with Jean Claude to clean the little creatures because this was definitely one cooking chore I could not do. Instead, I went out to our garden to pick some vegetables for dinner. Although I thought I had given the men plenty of time, I returned too soon. I entered the kitchen, followed by an unexpected gust of wind, and found myself covered in bird feathers!

While I brushed off the feathers outside, Jean Claude wrapped the birds in grape leaves and pancetta and drizzled them with farm fresh olive oil. He baked them to perfection.

Subsequent visits from Jean Claude enriched our dinner table with specialties of the French countryside: *pâté de champagne*, country-style *pâtés*, terrines of duck *foie gras*, and various other *charcuterie* specialties from his region. He always brought along Lautrec bread, baked in wood-burning ovens by local bakers, and a bottle of his homemade liqueur made from golden Mirabelle plums, whose trees blanket the fields along the pine forest of his country home.

When Jacque came to visit us from St. Jean de Luz, a seashore commune in the Pyrenees Atlantiques in southwestern France, he brought us gifts from the seaside region: three huge octopi. They were a size I had never seen sold commercially. The gleam in his eye showed his pride in being able to provide our dinner that night with his morning catch.

While the ugly creatures cooked in hot broth for our second course, Jacque prepared the first course of the evening meal, his rice specialty, *riso a nero* with black calamari sauce made from fresh squid ink he had brought from France. For the second course, he grilled the boiled octopus and spidery-looking tentacles. He completed our seafood feast with a ten-pound wheel of cheese, *Edelweise Fromage per Brebis,* made by the Basque people of his region. The pungent aromas of the sheep milk cheese permeated the air with each slice into the huge wheel. We spent the evening enjoying great food and regional music, and playfully painting our faces with squid ink as school children might do.

My mother introduced me to good olive oil over seventy years ago. I was just a baby, too young to know what I was eating, of course. But every Italian mother in those days would prepare a simple broth for their little ones: a simple vegetable stock made with fresh carrots, celery, and other vegetables along with *pastini* pasta and olive oil. It is a healthy dish, inexpensive, easy for a baby to digest, and a comfort food for all seasons, still practiced today.

Throughout my childhood, olive oil was always on the dinner table to enrich dishes and dinner salads. In addition to being used for cooking, olive oil had a multitude of uses and we never wasted a precious drop. If I had the flu, stomach cramps, indigestion, cold, or fever, a teaspoon of olive oil would be my medicine. If I was constipated, there was no question of its beneficial properties.

I hated hair-washing days when I was in elementary school. It meant that I had to sleep with my head bathed in olive oil, with my hair wound up and tucked into a plastic cap until morning. I often told my mom after shampooing my hair, "enough with this oil." My friends all used perfumed toiletries and hair products. I just had olive oil.

When I went off to college, I was able to escape my mother's insistence on this oily hair treatment and lavish my hair and skin with plenty of wonderful-smelling beauty products like my girlfriends did. I also learned to eat without olive oil on the table. Married life brought olive oil back into my kitchen. Later, when I moved to Italy, I found myself living on a farm with a grove of abandoned olive trees.

In 1985, Tuscany experienced the worst freeze in decades and many groves lost more than ninety percent of their trees. Ironically, our trees survived because they had been so neglected. They were covered with years of ragweed, tumbleweed, and unknown wild plants, which saved them from the devastating frost.

I was eager to clean up the grounds and develop my olive orchard. I had to prune the trees, clear the land, learn how to pick those tiny bitter fruits, and attempt to make that precious liquid my mother treated like gold.

I did everything wrong that first year. Seeing good olives on the ground, I proceeded to pick them up first, before climbing into the trees to get the olives clinging to their umbilical branches. A neighbor came by to check my work and told me how foolish I was to pick up the dropped olives, which were soiled and bruised. They were over-ripened, which would result in highly acidic, greasy oil with little nutritional value. He suggested that I pick the perfectly formed olives on the trees before they fell to the ground. I followed his advice, and began the laborious chore of handpicking every olive from our trees.

Wanting to make the best oil, I decided to spread my day's harvest onto a bedsheet on our dining room floor, which was devoid of furniture. I proceeded to remove all of the leaves, small twigs, and particles. Danny, a close friend and vice president of our bank, stopped by to see me. He chuckled and told me that I was wasting time picking out the leaves, because they would be discarded at the *frantoia*. Besides, if I continued working alone, it would take days to have enough to press, and by then the olives stored on the sheet would have increased their acidity, making poor quality oil. Danny suggested that I ask someone to help me harvest the olives.

I succeeded in getting help from our neighbor, and when we had collected enough olives for the press, we loaded my precious fruit into old burlap sacks and headed to the *frantoia*. This turned out to be another big no-no: packing olives in cloth sacks can increase the formation of mold. Most farmers carry their olives in colorful plastic crates, which are lightweight and have the advantage of allowing air to circulate.

I was compulsive about harvesting every olive. One day, six olives were just out of my reach. I held the trunk and leaned as far out as I could, but lost my balance, fell six feet down, and landed on a large exposed tree root. I was unable to sit for two weeks. At that point, I was almost ready to give up my foolish new endeavor. However, that evening, I read about a woman who was the oldest surviving human being in the world. Jeanne Calment of Arles, France, credited her age of one hundred twenty-two to a diet rich in olive oil. Any thoughts I'd had of quitting stopped right then and there.

That year, I went to the *frantoia* to press the sacks of my ugly looking, moldy, over-ripened, black, frostbitten olives. The olives were weighed, rinsed in a water bath, and put in a huge vat. Three six-hundred-pound granite wheels rolled around inside the vat and methodically crushed the olives into a paste. The paste was spread onto round, double-layered *fiscoli* mats woven from natural fibers. The mats had holes in the center and were stacked one on top of another onto a steel pillar. A hydraulic steel press then squeezed the *fiscoli*, allowing the oily liquid to run down the sides of the decanting tub.

A vertical centrifuge separated the natural vegetable oil from the residue of the fruit and from the unusable brownish-colored water. What was left on the fiscoli was a dry, tar-like black residue called pomace, which I had read was used as a natural fertilizer or for animal feed in Italy. My curiosity led me to ask the manager of the mill what he did with the pomace. With a smile on his face, he said "Pomace is used to make olive oil for the Americans. Huge manufacturing plants use heat and chemicals to process the residue into oil. You know Americans don't understand quality."

I set out to prove him wrong. Over time, I did extensive research, and the more I learned about olive oil, the more fascinated I became and I ascertained that the manager was right.

Olives have permeated Mediterranean culture since prehistoric times. The Romans were the first to use olive oil in cooking and invented the first press. Leonardo da Vinci invented the modern press, still used today. The Egyptian pharaohs moved stones to build the pyramids with the help of oil. Greek athletes used it to lubricate their muscles and light the Olympic flame; the champions received olive leaf crowns. A dove brought an olive branch to Noah on his ark as a sign of peace. Hercules' staff was an olive bough. Christ was nailed to a cross of olive wood. The Romans had a separate stock market just for oil, and spread knowledge of its culinary use throughout the Roman Empire. Before being consumed as a food item, it was used to beautify bodies, cure illnesses, moisturize skin, fill oil lamps and lubricate tools.

Mediterranean countries have been reaping the benefits of good olive oil for over two thousand years. It wasn't until the missionaries and immigrants, particularly Italians, planted olive trees in the 1800s that the New World began to appreciate the olive. Early attempts to produce olive oil resulted in an inferior product compared to what they were accustomed to in their homeland. This led to the conversion of olive groves into vineyards for making wine. The few olive trees that remained were left to produce what became the popular table olives.

In my youth in America, black olives were popular. These are actually green olives treated with acids and heat and packed in cans at various stages of ripeness. These olives are a popular snack and garnish, despite having little or no nutritional value. As for olive oil, for most Americans it continued to have little significance until the baby boomers began to realize its health benefits.

In May 2002, Dr. Walter Willett, professor and chair of the Department of Nutrition at the Harvard School of Public Health, was a special guest at a conference I attended in Bordeaux, France, with my daughter, Michelle. Considered an expert on fats and their effects on the body, he was one of the first to suggest that not all fats are bad, and encouraged the use of monounsaturated fats like olive oil.

Although Americans began to purchase olive oil for a healthier lifestyle, they had no idea what to consider when buying it. Olive-pomace is the product extracted from the olive pulp after the first press using chemical solvents. Since olive oil wasn't previously considered an important food item, this low-grade adulterated oil was labeled as "extra virgin" olive oil. It was exported to the United States and was popular in retail chain stores.

With unclear labeling and misunderstood descriptions, olive oil soon became one of the greatest frauds in the food business. Adulterated olive oil became commonplace in an unregulated and corrupt industry, resulting in cheaper oils being mislabeled and sold as "virgin" and "extra virgin" without the consumers'

Olive harvest

knowledge. Those who had the culture of oil could distinguish the difference; otherwise one would be fooled, as has occurred around the globe.

Truffle hunt

It has taken years for the U.S. government to realize the importance of this food item. More regulations are needed, but great steps have been taken to properly classify and control the olive oil industry. On August 7, 2015, Governor Jerry Brown and the California Legislature passed a bill, SB65: Food Labeling: Olive Oil, which requires manufacturers to accurately identify and label their olive oil blends, including the required percentages from regions and estates. My interest in olive oil led my husband and me to register for a professional olive oil sommelier course.

In April 2017, at Lake Garda, we received our diplomas as sommeliers after five days of testing over sixty samples and learning to detect the positive and negatives attributes of olive oil.

The farm has come a long way since my first amateur harvest. Guests arrive every fall to learn about olive oil and help with the annual olive harvest. From the harvest to storage in our cantina to shipping, we use stainless steel containers to best preserve our oil from light, sun, heat, and aromas that all effect the oil and lead it to rancidity.

Since olive harvesting occurs at the same time as the white truffle season, we organize truffle hunts. Following the truffleteur and his valuable trained dog through the woods in search of this ugly tuber is an enlightening experience. A successful hunt can be financially rewarding for the truffleteur, with truffles commanding anywhere from $1000 to $2000 dollars a pound. Class members love to experience the aroma of the fresh white truffle prized around the world, but regrettably they cannot take it home. Niece Kenzi wishes she could.

In addition to classes on making olive oil at Villa Lucia, we also offer an interesting class on making *balsamico di Modena*, a condiment not to be confused with balsamic vinegar. The only thing they have in common is that both are made from grapes. Balsamic vinegar is made with fermented grapes and additives including sugar, caramel, and molasses to give it flavor and masquerade its color.

Although many artisans are disappearing, families in Modena continue the centuries-long tradition of making *Traditionale Balsamico di Modena* (TBM). It was first used medicinally in 1046 to alleviate childbirth pain, and was auctioned as a luxury item during the French Revolution. In the 1800s, it was prized as a dowry item for girls, a  custom still followed by many families in Modena today. In 1912, Fini Federzoni of Modena began producing larger quantities, but it wasn't until 1980 that it became popular in the Western world, when chefs of *nouvelle cuisine* were seeking new flavors for their healthier creations and began using droplets of this expensive liquid to enrich their gourmet dishes.

Making authentic TBM begins with cooking white grapes like the *trebbiano*, a popular grape used in making chianti wine, in a stainless steel or copper cauldron over low heat. The product becomes caramelized, reduces by about fifty percent, and is left to rest for twenty-four hours. Then the carmalized *saba* begins its journey through the *batteria*, a row of between five and seven barrels of different sizes made from different woods, which influence the flavor of each batch.

The biggest cask, usually made of a hardwood live oak, receives the fresh batch of *saba*, where it begins the gradual acidification process. A small "bug" hole on the top of each barrel allows the *saba* to breathe and gives the maker control over the acidity.

This process takes place in well-ventilated *acetaia* (lofts or attics in private homes in Modena), which provide the contrasting temperatures required to make the finished product. Heat speeds up the evolution, while cold slows it

Niece Kenzi and her $500 truffle

down and stabilizes it. Gentle heat allows the yeast and microorganisms to survive. The gradual acidification in the barrels changes the color from amber to ebony, and a small percentage evaporates while aging. Over the course of the process, the sweet "must" changes into a condensed exotic combination of sweet and sour flavors.

After the minimum of twelve to twenty-five years, the TBM is tested and analyzed by a panel of expert judges who determine if the condiment can be given the TBM classification. If so, it goes into bulb-shaped bottles recognized around the world. The twelve-year product is distinguished by a silver top and the twenty-five-year type with a gold top. The condiment labels specify it as traditionale *balsamico di Modena* with the DOC seal *(Denominazione Originale Controllato)*. No two are alike due to differences in the production, use of woods, and the maker's skill. It is the only condiment in the world produced solely with cooked grapes and no additives. It is unfortunate that this condiment, TBM, is often referred to as vinegar, confusing the customer when the two items have nothing in common other than being made from grapes.

Return To Abruzzo

"To invite someone is to be responsible for his happiness as long as he is under your roof."

—Artusi

Having lived most of my life in two great countries, there came a time for my husband and me to decide where we would spend our last years. Both countries have their merits. America gave me my family, education, opportunity and freedom like no other country in the world. As a first-generation Italian-American, I succeeded in spite of few resources with which to fulfill the American Dream. But Italy gave me parents who enriched my life with what America did not give me, food culture. It wasn't until recently that I realized just how powerful and influential this component has been in determining who I am.

I am proud to have been born in the most dynamic, industrial country in the world, the United States of America. But I am also proud to be a daughter of hardworking Italian parents. The inherited molecules containing chromosomal material, which I call my "Italian DNA," are at the center of my heart and soul. My genes have influenced my emotional wellbeing, spirit, love of life, and desire to embrace the Italian lifestyle, which means enjoying the moment, life's simple pleasures, and conviviality with family and friends.

I have always loved the excitement of the big cities where I lived most of my adult life, so it took some effort to adjust to country life when we first moved to Tuscany in the 1980s. At first, it was strange listening to the cuckoo birds call to each other in the morning, the church bells chiming the hour, and the sounds of a distant tractor tilling the earth. The silence was even frightening at times, especially when I was alone. Before long, however, I came to respect the experience of having all of my senses in play. In our Italian farmhouse, I could see, hear, touch, smell, and taste the beauty of nature and all of its gifts.

After the slower pace of life in Tuscany, I found it difficult to return to the big cities I used to love when I was younger. Cities now leave me with a feeling of loneliness that prevails even in a crowd. Tension and stress have become commonplace in our fast-paced world. Now, whenever I visit cities, the country calls me to return.

My father often quoted Dante Alighieri, considered by many to be the greatest literary icon of the Western world and father of the Italian language. He combined Tuscan and other Italian dialects with Latin. In his essay on philosophy called "*Convivio*," Dante referred to a banquet of many courses, saying, "True nobility doesn't derive from heredity or possession of wealth but rather from the practice of virtue."

Father preached this to my sisters and me as well. We observed Dante's philosophy of life being practiced by our parents, country people who favored personal relationships over possessions. This was a factor when considering whether to retire to a small village like the ones I had experienced and loved in my youth.

Over the last thirty years in Tuscany, we have observed cultural changes as people have slowly adopted modern lifestyles. It has been disappointing to see many of our favorite family-run stores close due to the construction of giant commercial centers on the outskirts of Italian cities. These centers are having a major effect on daily life and on the traditional weekly farmers' markets that people depended on in the past. Restaurants in tourist areas, once open only for the midday meal, have been replaced by fast-food establishments to meet the needs of the tourists who prefer quick, inexpensive, all-day food service. I am saddened to see Italy starting to make adjustments like this, endangering its gastronomic culture.

Family-oriented activities like church, social clubs, and holiday gatherings are showing a decline in Italy as well. Here, as in the U.S., dual-income families find it difficult to balance family obligations, and that adds stress to everyday life.

Tuscany will always be special to us. The wonderful friends we have made at Villa Lucia have enriched our lives, and the memorable gatherings on the farm

with family and friends, eating *al fresco* among the olive trees against a background of unforgettable sunsets and sunrises, will remain in our heart.

However, managing a villa and its 15 acres as a forty-year-old may not be difficult, but when approaching the age of eighty and ninety, we realize it is time to leave management to others. We hope to continue to enjoy *convivio*, now dividing our time between the two regions we love, Tuscany and Abruzzo, the unspoiled heart of the Italian peninsula, where the north meets the south, a paradise of authenticity.

Being geographically separated for centuries from the rest of Italy by the Adriatic Sea on the east and the Apennine Mountains on the west, the people of Abruzzo haven't been exposed to modern life, so their cultural traditions remained intact longer than most. In 1968, it took us six hours to get to Rome from the home of my maternal grandfather. Today, with the new superhighway built in the late 1980s, it takes just an hour.

Abruzzo's three mountain regions, Gran Sasso, Maiella, and Laga, separate the Adriatic Sea from the Tyrrhenian Coast and remain one of the least-developed regions of Italy, with a third of the region devoted to national and regional parks. This makes it a paradise for nature lovers and a place where it's possible to step back in time to a traditional Italian lifestyle. This region has some of the most spectacular scenery in Italy: awe inspiring mountains, wooded areas of solitude, verdant gentle rolling hills, unspoiled medieval hill towns, and warm sandy beaches.

Parents and maternal grandpa in Rome, 1947

Standing on top of the Gran Sasso, the Apennines' highest mountain, one can view both the Adriatic and the Tyrrhenian Seas across the entire width of Italy, with vistas of authentic wilderness, landscapes of wild mountains and rolling hills

where wolves and bears still roam. These mountains provide great ski slopes in the winter and offer great hiking and climbing in relative solitude throughout the year. The mountains are home to deer, chamonix, foxes, and wolves that roam in the forests of chestnut, beech, and oak trees. In 1917, the first proposal for creating the national parks in Abruzzo was made with the aim of improving and maintaining the fauna and rich flora, which included a wide range of trees and medicinal plants. The area was the natural reserve for the royal families who used to come from Rome to hunt bears and chamonix. In 1923, Il Parco Nazionale d'Abruzzo, the largest park in Europe, was established to save the brown bear and chamonix from extinction as well as to preserve the beautiful countryside.

The Gran Sasso mountain range, Italy's largest, includes the Corno Grande, the highest peak of the Apennine. Its eastern side, with a wild landscape of jagged peaks, ridges, and spectacular steep chalky rock rises sharply from the hilly countryside, creating an Alpine landscape. In contrast, on its western side, there is the Campo Imperatore, a plateau 30 km long and 8 km wide, often referred to as "little Tibet." It has been the ideal setting for various movie backdrops, particularly spaghetti Westerns. Today, it is being discovered and is becoming a paradise for hikers and cross-country skiers, as well as for snowshoe expeditions. With its breathtaking beauty, from the Campo Imperatore plateau one can gain access to the eternal snow of the Calderone, Europe's southernmost glacier. Few realize unless visiting the Campo Imperatore Hotel, which I did with Francesco and Laila, that it was there in 1943 that German paratroopers performed one of their most dangerous yet amazing and successful operations when they freed Mussolini from captivity.

The magnificent Abruzzese coastline also offers a varied terrain. In the north, the flat, smooth inlets and sandy beaches are popular for families with children  and swimmers seeking calm waters. The south, also known as the Trabocco Coast, has cliffs and rocky promontories that jut out into the sea. This area has the ancient and ingenious il trabocco (fishing machine platform) constructed out of wood and anchored to the rocks. Fishermen used long wooden poles and an elaborate set of winches, ropes and pulleys to lower fishing nets into the sea and raised them full of the day's catch. The spidery structures look a bit precarious jutting out into the sea, but they have withstood centuries of violent storms. Regional laws protect these national monuments, and UNESCO has listed these historical remains as world cultural heritage sites. The peculiar wooden dwellings stretching between Ortona and San Salvo have been converted into restaurants serving fresh seafood and *convivio* style dining.

Trabocco

Abruzzo's ancient ruins date back to Roman times with medieval villages still intact. A leader in preserving its history and culture, Abruzzo has created stringent laws to save the old towns and villages along with its rocky promontories of castles, hermitages, fortified settlements, abbeys, and archaeological sites. These laws provide a balance between traditional and modern life. Use of local stone makes new construction harmonious with the existing structures. The stone is also used in landscaping, so castles and homes blend seamlessly into the hillsides. There are more castles in Abruzzo than in any other region of Italy. Pacentro, a gem of a town at the foot of Mount Morrone, is best known for its medieval castle. I attended my cousin's wedding in this castle, built in about 1000 AD. His family, the Marquis of Introdacqua, was forced to move to Sulmona when the Germans took over the town during WWII, using it as their headquarters.

Their villa stands empty today, like many of the local homes that were vacated during the war. Today, Pacentro is attracting many foreigners interested in buying a piece of this historical village.

Enjoying convivio in a trabocco

One of my favorite castles is Rocca Calascio, a castle at 1500 meters above sea level at the top of a cliff on the edge of Campo Imperatore. It is the oldest and highest fort in Italy and originally served as a watchtower in the tenth century. It has been the site for many film productions such as *Ladyhawke* with Michelle Pfeiffer and sequences of *The Name of the Rose* and *The American* with George Clooney, and National Geographic selected it as one of the top ten castles in the world. Granddaughter Laila enjoying the view as royalty may have done.

The castle became the central base of the *via della lana* (wool roads) for the traditional *transumanza*, the springtime herding of sheep from the lowlands to higher mountain pastures. Watchful sheep herders guide the flocks across the land. Grandsons Dante and Luca enjoyed a day with their parents and one of the last shepherds.

When my cousin Gabrielle invited me to join him and fifty-five others on a short *transumanza* along the Morrone mountain trails, part of the Appenines, I jumped at the opportunity.

Using handy walking sticks, we hiked behind a herd of eight hundred sheep through breathtaking pastures, green hills, and mountains. The pace was leisurely,

as the sheep stopped to eat along the way. The trained Abruzzese *maremmano* sheep dogs are massive white dogs with distinctive bear-like heads. They worked under the direction of the shepherd's master dog to protect the sheep and the shepherd from predators. The dogs would spread out along the hillside and guard the area. If a sheep deviated from the trail, the shepherd would give a command and the lead dog would run like the wind and guide the sheep back to the flock. The crown on the *maremmano's* neck acts as a protection for fighting wolfs.

Built by the shepherds and farmers of Abruzzo hundreds of years ago, the *tholos*, conical structures of stones, provided protection from the elements. Having existed since Paleolithic times, *tholos* were built in Abruzzo by the transumanti shepherds.

The *tholos* (tombs) were encircled by stone walls to protect the flocks of sheep and goats from wolves. During the Bronze Age, the Greeks adopted the conical construction shape, giving it the name *tholos*. Hand set stones formed a large

circular base. Carefully set layers gradually built upon each other in smaller and smaller circles, until the structure was complete. A small opening served as the only entrance. A wood burning pit in the center and stones to sit on provided the only comforts to the occupants.

Today, the few remaining tholos are scattered on the Maiella, the second highest mountain of the Appennines range, with its massive slopes, valleys and gorges. Some have been fortified and are used by locals as storage for agricultural equipment, barns, and tourist attractions. While walking along an old transumanza path, my husband and I once found an ancient, caved-in tholo. Just as I climbed in, my husband shouted, "Lucy! Get out!" I quickly scrambled out. Little did I know that abandoned *tholos* had become havens for vipers and other creatures!

Today's undiscovered treasures of Abruzzese gastronomy are the same foods that were on my family's table in the 1940s. The farms are organic, as they were then, except now they are certified. In the past, it was a way of life, not a specialty. My relatives continue to eat seasonal, healthy, locally grown food. They serve food like freshly made pigeon or chicken soup, fresh trout from the lake, and homemade pastas stuffed with ricotta and spinach. With a long history of shepherding, the popular meat dishes in the mountain area are lamb, goat, and mutton. In addition, these animals provide milk to make a wide variety of regional cheese.

The elders continue to maintain cellars full of aged cheeses and homemade salami that always come handy for a quick dinner or unexpected guests, just as in my youth in Connecticut. Meals usually end with the serving of fresh fruit followed by an espresso or homemade liqueur. Indulging in sweet desserts is reserved for guests and or special occasions, but *pizzelli*, the traditional Abruzzese cookies, are still made in Abruzzo as they were in the 1700s.

The waffle-like cookies are made on a hot iron press on the stove. The cast iron press usually has the family's initials on one side and the year the iron press was made on the other. My mother's press was a wedding gift in 1932 and included my father's initials, "A.V.," for Attilio Vallera. Although the thick waffle cookie is most often flavored with anise, my mother also made them with orange and lemon zest. Today, electric presses have replaced the personalized irons of the past and produce a thinner wafer, but the three-hundred-year-old tradition of *pizzelli*-making continues.

There are other unique regional specialties as well. Few realize that the world's most expensive spice, saffron, is grown in the Navelli plains of Abruzzo. Alleged to have been brought to Abruzzo by a Dominican monk named Santucci from Spain some 1300 years ago, it was originally appreciated for its antiseptic and digestive medicinal properties. Today, the dried and ground stems are used as a culinary spice to flavor and color dishes. Although the ground form is expensive, the precious and more aromatic red stigma stems cost about ten times more.

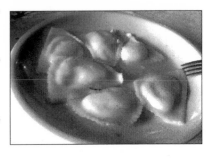

Saffron is grown in a few other areas of Italy, but the Abruzzese quality is known for being the best due to its long stigma stems, superior strong-perfumed aroma, and deep profound color. The saffron harvest takes place in October, early in the morning, before the six purple petals of each flower open to expose the delicate red stigmas. The harvest is labor intensive; it takes about 200,000 flowers to make a kilo of saffron. Immediately following the harvest, skilled workers delicately free the stigmas from each flower. The stigmas are heated to dry. A good day's work may produce a mere one hundred grams. The saffron represents the true symbol of Abruzzese tradition. Popular are pasta dishes with saffron.

Abruzzo is also well known for its *macharoni alla chitarra* pasta, usually served with a typical Abruzzo sauce, such as *carbonara* or a lamb *ragu*. The *chitarra* is a harp-like pasta cutter with a hard wooden frame and adjustable cast aluminum wires, which cuts the pasta dough into strips. My cousins make pasta this way, and I have introduced this method of pasta-making in our cooking classes as well. Supposedly, this excellent artisanal pasta has its origin in Pratola Peligna, home to my ancestors and the Masciarelle family. Since 1867, they have been using the same artistic technique to passionately produce artisan pastas.

A meal with a group of friends may end with *la coppia dell' amicizia*, the friendship cup, being passed around the table for all the guests to sip. The friendship cup is a wide, shallow wooden bowl with a round lid usually carved with beautiful scenes of flowers or animals. It has many spouts, depending on the size of *la coppa*, from which each guest takes a sip and passes it on to the next guest on the right. Folklore says that putting it down or touching the table will bring bad luck. It is another way of prolonging *convivio* at the table with friends and family and to finish each meal with laughter. Each sip brings heat, comfort, and cheer.

Sharing the hot, comforting contents of the friendship cup is especially popular in the cold northern regions. Although not commonly practiced in Abruzzo, I love the conviviality it provides. The most popular drinks are either hot wine, like a *vin brule,* made with spices such as cinnamon, nutmeg, and citrus zest, or hot strong coffee with *grappa*, sugar, and citrus. We have often enjoyed experiencing this after-dinner pleasure, passing a *coppia* with guests before happily retiring for the night.

Abruzzo has a long history of wine-making in ancient cellars, and is the fifth most productive region in Italy. Being geographically cut off from other popular wine-producing regions like Tuscany and Lazio, Abruzzo produces its own unique

1947

wine. Due to its favorable yield, Abruzzo exports twice as much wine as Tuscany, despite having less than thirty-eight percent vineyard land. The most renowned wines are the deep red DOC graded *Montelpuciano d'Abruzzo* and the white DOC *Trebbiano d'Abruzzo,* which was named the best in Italy in 2012. A popular rosé, Cerasuolo, made also from the Montepulciano grape, is deep red in color, yet spends less time in maceration before the pressing than most rosés. It is a hearty rosé with the aromas of cherries and exotic spices.

Many of the Abruzzo relatives who gave me so many wonderful memories of enjoying foods together at the family table have long since passed. But I am happy

2018

to see their children continue to enjoy the Italian tradition of eating and living. They believe, as their elders did, that besides food, the two most important ingredients for an enjoyable meal are family and friends at the table. Sitting with my cousins, long gone, I now enjoy the same villa, the same table with their grandchildren, our third cousins. The importance of the table is reinforced in the Italian language with two distinct definitions of the word. The feminine form, *la tavola*, is the experience and life at the table, whereas the masculine form, *il tavolo*, refers to the actual piece of furniture.

My life in Abruzzo today brings back many memories of my childhood in America. On Sundays, we all gathered around the family table, and were often joined by extended family members and friends, all compatriots from Abruzzo. With over 5,000 immigrants from the same region in Italy who settled in our Connecticut community, we had weddings, birthdays, baby showers, and funerals to attend every weekend. I loved these gatherings as a child because they gave me opportunities to socialize with other children whose parents also maintained the tradition and culture of the old world.

Having experienced these events in my youth in Connecticut makes me feel very much at home when in Abruzzo. As children, the highlight of the year was the first Sunday in May, when we would celebrate our patron saint at the feast of the *Madonna Della Libera di Pratola Peligna*. Pratola is the town where my ancestors, grandparents, parents, and sister Rose were born. As a child, I counted the days leading up to this great celebration, when *paesani* scattered in other American communities would travel to Connecticut to honor their patron saint and unite with compatriots. Today, in Italy, this tradition continues, and I still enjoy the festivities with friends and family.

Rarely missing from any festivity, *sagra*, religious event, or gathering of family and friends was the Abruzzese *arrosticini*. Skewers are packed with a dozen or so small pieces of lamb and cooked over an open fire to succulent crispy perfection. Today a *braciere*, a long and narrow horizontal grill, is used to cook large quantities.

It is a delicious, fun, healthy and light appetizer enjoyed by all. The kind of meat is often specified for the consumer.

Jorge and I wish to enjoy new and old friends and continue to give our children some of the traditions I was fortunate to have experienced in Abruzzo, as we did in Tuscany. Our new residence will be an old stone house with crooked, bulging walls, without a single ninety-degree corner. Yet I love this house because its stone walls have survived a thousand years of nature's unpredictable weather conditions.

The farmer who built our house centuries ago clearly knew how to construct it to keep the cold out in the winter and the heat out in the summer. The design includes a *grotta*, or underground cave, like most homes in the area. The *grottas* once served as shelters for small family animals, protecting them from foul weather and allowing them to be close enough to be cared for. The *grotta* also served as a cantina for making and storing wine, and as storage for products needing a cool environment before refrigeration was available. On unbearable hot summer days, the *grottas* provided a cool and comfortable refuge for family and friends as well.

When visiting, I love to take advantage of the knowledge of the few remaining elders to learn the history of our village, which is made up of stone houses and their *grottas* surrounding a medieval tower that sits high above the village and was used in the past to warn the inhabitants of approaching invaders. Many of the residents shared their interesting tales of life in the *grottas*, some happy, but a number of them sad, especially when describing the role the grottas served during the war.

One day, I was working at the house when a gentleman in his eighties walked by and told me that he had grown up in our house. I invited him in and was proud to show him my work in progress. He seemed pleased with our renovation plans, but his smile of approval vanished when we reached our grotta. His eyes welled with tears as he told me that during the war, the grotta's main purpose was to serve as a hiding place from the German troops. His parents had piled horse manure and other animal excrement at least two feet into the arched *grotta* entrance to hide their children behind the repellent pile of stench. As little children, they had to learn to be silent in spite of their foul-smelling, manure-covered clothing and surroundings.

Putting an arm around his shoulder, I told him that I hoped he would visit sometime again soon, joining others in my *grotta* and making it a place of happy encounters for him.

Our small home is designed to encourage everyone to congregate and interact in the kitchen\living room. There are no big bedrooms for sleeping, no large bathrooms to clean, no yard to tend, no lawn to mow, no walls to paint, and no office full of paperwork to do. It is the kitchen that brings the family together.

The most important pieces of furniture in our kitchen, living room, dining room, and *grotto* are the tables. They are oversized for the rooms to accommodate family and friends, encouraging communication and *convivio*. Our table seats fourteen; the table is of greater importance in our family than having a big TV.

When we bought our California home in 1970, my husband informed our children that there would be no televisions, telephones, or radios in their bedrooms. He believed these items prevented interaction and limited conversations. We had our only television in the family room for all to share.

Being new to California in the 1970s, our dining room table became the setting for weekend dinners with new acquaintances. It didn't take long for our dining room table to bring us a large community of friends from all walks of life. Over the years, many of these same people visited us in Tuscany, where they had had the opportunity to enjoy our Tuscan table, which comfortably seats twenty-five people. Many went home after visiting us to buy a new table or modify their existing one to accommodate more guests, then wrote to us about their experiences, even sharing some of their table designs.

I had no idea, when I first began inviting guests to Italy, that our time at the table would be a new experience for many of them, as confirmed by the many letters we have received from guests who were eager to share how they changed their lifestyle at home after enjoying *convivio* with us in Tuscany:

Dear Lucy,

I was always longing for one long table where we could all sit together side by side. A trip to Villa Lucia in 2009 opened my eyes to how much fun this could be and repeated trips convinced me it wasn't a coincidence—no matter who was at the table the conversation was lively and the time flew

by—no one ever wanted to be the first to leave. When we were looking for a new home, I knew I wanted a place for a table like the one at Villa Lucia—I got my wish. Thanks Lucy and Jorge for all you have given to us—you showed me the way!

Maile

<hr />

Dear Lucy,

The story that I usually tell describes how we were first introduced to your table the first night of our first visit at Villa Lucia. We had arrived late from Florence, so we took a quick shower and walked into your backyard where a large group was gathered, and where you welcomed us to join them for dinner. We knew no one there, but by the end of the evening, we were all friends. We had never heard about convivio, but we experienced it that evening. Your table was unbelievable, and I recall reaching for the lazy susan in the center several times for another helping of your famous white beans, or another glass of wine. The evening was absolutely enchanting!

Since we had just built a Tuscan-styled outdoor kitchen, and loved to entertain large groups, I had to have a "Lucia's table." However, while there was room in the yard, I wanted it adjacent to the kitchen on a patio... which I had to build first. So right after we returned from our month with you in 2013, I started building the patio, preparing a foundation, and then placing by hand, about five hundred paving stones (as shown in one of the above photos). That winter, I started on the table in my shop, so that it would be ready the following summer, 2014.

I had investigated a granite slab top, which would have been in two pieces because of the large size. But that would have made the table a monument, never to be moved (like yours!), and we wanted to have the patio available for dancing too. So I decided to build the top of

wood in four quadrants, and have the base fabricated from steel, with wooden legs that I built to match the top. The table can be disassembled in the off-season for storage, but it's a two-person job to get it set up! Since the above pictures were taken, I've completed a lazy susan for the top. It alone is five feet in diameter.

I had a table dedication party last summer. Before we sat down, I read a few excerpts from your book draft about Convivio, and explained how your table inspired me to build this ten-foot-diameter table. On the underside of one of the tabletop quadrants, I wrote a special dedication to you. I plan to affix a more permanent nameplate.

Everyone loves to eat around our table, and loves the story that goes with it. Every time we host a table-full of guests, I feel like we've shared a little bit of Tuscany, Villa Lucia, and Lucy with everyone, and shown them a little Convivio!

We love you, and will keep you in our prayers.

George Tocquigny

Dear Lucy and Jorge

"A visit that inspired us to rethink our lifestyle"

Shall never forget our first visit with you at Villa Lucia with my wife and family. We returned home to California incredibly inspired. Our stay was truly one of the best experiences of our life and influenced some major life changes. We were so enamored by the magical grounds filled with an olive orchard, vegetable gardens, and amazing flowers, the property an Old World gem.

Your cooking lessons were the best part. We loved preparing the nightly meal with vegetables right out of the garden, and learning the real Italian classics, letting everyone participate. Then the topper was dining at your huge table which accommodated over 14 of us. Such an amazing experience! It was so heart-warming that you instantly became family to us and hope we shall always be in contact with each other.

Our visit inspired us so greatly, we returned home and instantly incorporated the nightly dining by remodeling our dining room to accommodate a new large dining table for large groups as experienced with you. After six months of our visit we decided to move out of Laguna Beach and buy a vineyard in

the central coast of California which also included an olive orchard. We designed our new home to accommodate a large dining table and kitchen and styled it with a total Tuscan theme.

So you see, this one trip to Villa Lucia and meeting you two great people has had a major impact on our lives forever. Thank you Lucy and Jorge.

Rich Secchiaroli

◆━◆◆◆◆━◆

Lastly, is a very touching story I would like to convey of a wonderful and talented artist who would bring groups of friends and professors from Indianapolis on a regular basis. Claiming that he had every art book possible, I gave him a surprise birthday party and gave him a book of the erotic art of Pompeii. One he surely did not have. We have had so many wonderful times together that it broke my heart when his wife Peggy wrote that before he died, he wanted to paint his last picture of Villa Lucia. On his last trip he presented it to me. On his last birthday, he wrote such a beautiful letter and asked if his daughter Jamie could bring his ashes to Villa Lucia, regretting that I was not there for his last birthday. I am honoring his wish. Jamie will be coming this year. This will be the seventh guest whose ashes have been carried back to Italy to rest by Villa Lucia. It is an honor to do this. I am looking forward to meeting the daughter he spoke so highly of during many nights of *convivio* dinners. I could not complete this book without presenting a reflection of his letter upon dying and what it means to me and my family. Guests such as Paul and Peggy Sweaney have enriched my life with a treasure chest of great memories to cherish.

For most Italians, the table is the place of love and friendship. Sadly, many Americans do not understand the merits of the family table like we do. The table gave our children some of their best memories. When we moved from our California home in the

Introdacqua

early 1990s, our youngest son Jason asked us to please not sell the table that held so many memories, so it traveled with us from California to Tuscany. Now, years later, it has traveled with us to Abruzzo, where it sits in our little stone house, ready to add to the memories.

We decided to settle in Introdacqua, a medieval *borgo* in the Valle Peligna in the heart of Abruzzo, where some of my ancestors immigrated from and where others have remained. Coincidentally, the most impressive remaining historic building in this town is the Marquis Trasmondi Palace, once the home of my cousin's grandmother, the Marchesia Nicola Maria. I feel fortunate to have spent time with her, one of the last of the Marchesia's grandchildren. When Italy was united as a country in the late 1800s, feudal lordships were repealed, and the Marquisate of the Transmondis came to an end. The family moved to Sulmona, where many of my relatives live today, just a few miles outside of the little *borgo* of Introdacqua.

The palace in Introdacqua, covering an area of about seven hundred fifty square meters, catered large political and social events in its magnificent halls for over five hundred years. The terraces offer breathtaking views of the rich agricultural land. The Trasmondi Palace has been established as a monument of historical significance, and the stories of families that lived within its walls will be preserved for generations to come.

Cousin's wedding in Pacentro castle

Our town, with fewer than two thousand habitants, is peaceful except during the summer months, when the world seems to come for cool evenings and cultural events. The village of Introdacqua gets its name, which means "between the waters," from its location. Endless falls of mountain water from the Apennines

cascade every day of the year down to the town, supplying the community with fresh water. The mountain air, clean and invigorating, complements the delicious fresh mountain water, creating a recipe for clean living and longevity.

While moving some of our furnishings into our stone house, I discovered the Locanda dei Asini, a donkey farm just a few minutes from our home. Since then, I have enjoyed visiting the descendants of my grandpa's donkey Bella, who had given me some of my best childhood memories in Abruzzo.

On one particular visit, after watching the children trekking with the donkeys, we were impressed to see the children making focaccia for lunch. Mothers and teachers helped the children and an employee cooked the focaccia in a wood-burning pizza oven. It was wonderful to see children preparing their own lunch and appreciating the work involved.

Sulmona, the main town outside of Introdacqua, allows access to modern necessities of life just a few miles away. It is a beautiful medieval town, famous for being the hometown of the Latin poet Ovidio, born in 43 AD. Visitors come for its medieval cathedral, beautiful churches, and its twenty-one well-preserved medieval aqueduct arches. The annual jousting competition takes place in the central Piazza Garibaldi, encircled by the aqueduct.

Sulmona is a very cultural and historical city, referred to as "the city of art." Although known for its artisans of yesterday, such as goldsmiths, copper and iron smiths, and embroiderers, Sulmona is best known as *"la citta dei confetti,"* the local confectionery craftsmanship of *"confetti"* sugared almonds, uniquely valued and recognized throughout the world. A symbol of fortune and prosperity since Roman times, they continue to be present at any special family event in the form of *bonbonieres* or party favors. When my son married, little tulle bags of *confettis* were wrapped around our olive oil bottles and given as *bonboniere*, as practiced by our Abruzzese ancestors.

In my youth, relatives visiting us in America always brought beautifully decorated objects made with various kinds of colorful confetti. These colorful works of art often were displayed for months before we were allowed to enjoy eating them. They are mass-produced in the U.S. (commonly called Jordan almonds), but I believe these lack the quality and taste of the Italian sweets, especially the delicate candy shell.

In our little town of Introdacqua, there is still a vibrant community family life, especially among the elders. When a local mason was offered four times his salary to move elsewhere, he refused. He said he would miss his friends, community, after-lunch coffee with the guys, his game of cards after dinner, safe daily walks through town with his grandchildren, wine-making in the fall, *prosciutto*-making in the winter, and all the social, religious, and cultural events he had been attending with his *paesani* since he was a child. His wife would continue to want to make her canned goods and meet with her friends after church for coffee in the *piazza*. For them, life in their community had no substitute.

My hairdresser was offered an opportunity to go to America, and I was surprised to hear that he had refused. I understood better when I saw his three-year-old enter the beauty salon while I was getting a haircut. The entire staff stopped their work to hug, kiss, and greet the little one, asking him for a *bacino, bacino, bacino* (little kiss). His children are loved by the entire community. They can play in the street and walk home alone, knowing that someone in the community is watching them and will be there to protect them, as if the child were a blood relative.

An amazing artisan carpenter told me he did not wish to bring his family to America either. "How could I live apart from my friends?" he asked me. Where would he go when he wanted a moment of solitude outdoors? Now he can walk to his farm near his home to be absorbed in the beauty of the countryside and be rewarded with products produced by his passion for woodworking and gardening.

Convivio of 53 neighbors on our patio

Many of these people in Abruzzo and the surrounding areas are free of the stress of long commutes to get to work. Cars aren't even necessary in these old villages. Many towns in Italy are designed for people, not cars, and a family can easily adapt to a one-car household. In most modern cities, the car is of such importance, especially for getting to work and school, that a one-car household is often unrealistic. This can negatively affect finances and family time, as having multiple cars adds stress to both. In Introdacqua, public transportation is so good that one is not cut off even from big city excitement. Rome is but ninety minutes away via public transportation. It is a pace of life not easily found elsewhere. Introdacqua is also a community where people intermingle. Foreigners and Italians join together

American and Italian cousins joined the group

in the festivities, work projects, and life in the *piazza*. The summer months bring tourists to the town square every night to enjoy music and cultural programs of every kind. Emigrants from throughout the world return for those summer days in Introdacqua. Weekly *sagras*, or food fairs, and various religious festivals provide social opportunities requiring little or no money to attend. It is an opportunity to get together as we are here on our patio with our American and Italian neighbors. Our home is the meeting place for our American and Italian cousins to get together.

The Italian character of excelling in communicating is ingrained in their culture and leads to *"l'arte d'arrangiamento,"* the skill to solve problems. In the Italian family, there appear to be fewer conflicts between children and parents than in other European countries due in part to a tenacious family loyalty. The family provides a network of the deepest and most important relationships in Italian society. There is no social stigma attached to having three generations living under one roof.

My family has continued this tradition. My sisters and I were fortunate to have our grandfather living with us during our youth. Our children had three grandparents living with them on a rotating schedule in our California home. Neighbors sometimes asked how we could tolerate living with our extended family, but for us it was a normal and wonderful thing to share life together. It is this strong family bond that builds a resistance to the evolution of unfavorable behaviors and ensures quality of life.

On hot summer nights in August, the town square of Introdacqua is full of people until the wee hours of the morning. Relatives who have emigrated to other countries often return in August. Locals from surrounding towns visit in the evenings, since the hot days of summer are cooler in Introdacqua, where mountain breezes make the evenings comfortable. I am always amazed to see the young children under eight playing soccer in the square at midnight and infants awake in carriages, having obviously had a siesta with the family during the heat of the summer day. The entire town gathers in the small town square and everyone seems to know everyone else. The atmosphere is relaxed and comfortable. Teenagers walk up and down the main street, usually in groups, stopping to talk with others along the way. They are usually the last to leave the square, walking safely home even late at night or in the early hours of morning.

One evening, as I was sipping a cup of tea with friends at one in the morning, I was surprised to hear the sounds of a local youth band marching down the street. The music caught the attention of all the locals, who left their seats at the outdoor cafés to see what was going on. They began playing "Happy Birthday" and the townspeople joined in singing "*auguri*" to the birthday person. A big cake in the center of the square informed us that it was for a young man of thirty-seven with Down Syndrome. The unexpected outpouring of affection was emotional, especially for him. The children of the town danced and people watched from their balconies as the youth band played music and brought smiles and laughter to the entire community.

In our small villages, it is considered bad etiquette if one walks down the street and does not greet everyone they encounter. One of the few drawbacks is that you can't get a lot done. If you walk down the street, everyone stops you along the way. Purchasing a loaf of bread might take you the entire evening. People love socializing and going out for a walk or coffee, always finding someone to accompany them. Although Italians love to eat together, restaurants are not as popular in villages, except for special occasions. People prefer to eat in family kitchens, where family and friends work together to prepare the meal as they talk, drink, and enjoy each other's company.

Every August, Sulmona has its own panarda, the multicourse feast of robust mountain dishes carved in my memory. One year, I invited twenty American and Italian friends to join me for what turned out to be their first panarda. The panarda held at the Largo Palizze Piazza in Sulmona did not go on until morning as was done in the 1940s, and was modified to have twenty dishes instead of fifty. But, as I had experienced in the past, time flew by quickly. The one hundred fifty guests were entertained by a spectacular program of medieval performances

between each course. There were falconers with trained birds, dancers, musicians, and theatrical performers beautifully dressed in colorful medieval costumes providing entertainment in the center of the piazza. Teams of five waiters in costumes traveled the room carrying enormous five-by-two-foot wooden serving boards, with two waiters to hold each end and a third to serve each course. The nobility, dressed in elegant costumes of rich fabrics, were seated facing the entertainment in the center.

I feel very much at home, returning to my roots and living in a place where the traditions of the past live on, infusing the present with a rich sense of artistry and color.

The "No Time" Virus

The Beginning of the Decline of Simple Pleasures, 1920 Genuine Food, 2020 *Convivio*

"Respect your dinner, idolize it, enjoy it, enjoy it properly. You will be many hours in the week, many weeks in the year, and many years in your life happier if you do."

–WILLIAM THACKERAY

The decline of genuine foods in America seems to have begun during the 1920s. The family dinner hour was still a priority back then and family bonds and traditions remained strong, even as processed foods and time-saving devices became popular. Over the next hundred years, however, genuine foods, family bonds, traditions, and culture seemed to lose importance at an alarming pace, particularly during the post-war years. Farmers after the war were able to obtain cheap fossil fuel, which became the base for new chemical fertilizers and pesticides, which in turn enabled the production of greater quantities of foods. Simultaneously, canned items gained popularity, along with a cornucopia of prepared and processed foods. This new cuisine of time-saving products proved to be a profitable endeavor for the food industry and marked the era where time in the kitchen and at the table became scarce.

Today, the Italian woman, like the American woman, typically works outside the home and finds herself juggling parenting, household, and work responsibilities. Although she may adopt some of the shortcuts in cuisine, purchasing from *la tavola calda* (hot meals prepared to go) and hurrying to complete chores on an overbooked calendar of activities, she continues as taught by her ancestors to seek out quality foods and maintain *convivio*. With her leisure time at a minimum, she is more apt to eliminate other activities before eliminating family time at the table.

The belief in our modern society is that multitasking increases efficiency, but often this results in a loss of pleasure. Movies romanticize Europeans relaxing in a café, sipping their morning coffee before going off to work. In contrast, the Americans are seen rushing to work with coffee in hand.

In Italy, speed and food are not meant to coincide. Italians view food not only as a nutritional delivery system of vitamins, minerals and energy, but as a medium to provide pleasure, satisfy their appetites, and fulfill complex cultural and social needs. They enjoy simple pleasures related to discovering quality foods: searching for asparagus in the woods, seeking out the best local producers, and organizing family outings and projects around food. The American public is slowly focusing on healthier foods, but just as important should be the emphasis on enjoying leisurely meals, eating together with families and friends, and teaching our children good culinary habits. If practiced on a daily basis, the vicious circle of high stress, fast food, and fast living will be replaced by the Italian way of living life.

In spite of the recent emphasis on eating well in America, this country continues to value quantity and novelty over quality. The French love their brioches and croissants. The Italians love their pizza and cornets. These two countries have food culture, and for them there is no substitute for quality.

Meanwhile, Americans are embracing hybrid foods—foods modified to create unique food items for profit, regardless of the health consequences. In 1910, the German hotdog was combined with Mexican chili to make a hybrid, the first chilidog, which was fine. A Belgium waffle is a good breakfast item, but is it necessary to deep fry it, top it with icing, and add colorful sprinkles to make a *Wonut*? Must croissant dough be fried to become a cronut? What about a burrito stuffed with a glazed donut? Or a donut stuffed with ice-cream? How about a pizza bagel? What's next? Unfortunately, these hybrids often come at the expense of the customer's health.

Unfortunately, despite the increasing popularity of the Mediterranean diet, adherence to it is on the decline. Other influences, such as economic and socio-cultural factors, lifestyle changes, and food globalization have posed serious threats to the preservation and transmission of this model of healthy eating.

Studies have determined that countries practicing the Mediterranean diet are changing and adopting more American-style eating habits. This is devastating, especially considering the decline may be irreversible. In Greece, thirty percent, and in Spain, fifty percent no longer adhere to a Mediterranean diet. Thanks to the tradition of the family table, Italy has been able to maintain the Mediterranean diet and *convivio* lifestyle longer than other countries, but changes are gradually taking place here as well. Tourism is also largely to blame as travelers seek out fast-food establishments.

When it comes to *convivio*, I believe the future is bleak unless we take deliberate action to once again put a priority on life around the table with friends and family. The decline of family bonding, traditional foods, and other cultural shifts in the name of "efficiency" have instigated an epidemic of unprecedented social problems. Single parent households in the 1960s made up about nine percent of the total. Today, about thirty-five percent of families are headed by single parents, usually women. A single parent often finds it difficult to establish the magically shared moments that dining together around a table can provide. Two-parent families may be more likely to have a dinner hour, but most have become so obsessed with work and a full calendar of activities for the children that the dinner hour is no longer a priority. Society has accepted the "no time" excuse when it comes to cooking and eating, and table time has become less important.

Doing sports and going to the gym are beneficial to one's well-being, but athletes' diets often consist of healthy drinks, meal substitute protein bars, vitamin pills, fiber bars, and individually packaged diet foods. They are becoming the norm for the "no time" virus. Tired of the sweetened diet bars and bored with eating the same thing, athletes are now seeking more savory items. This new demand has revolutionized the snack food industry. Gels and bars are being made to taste like popular foods: pizza, sweet potato French fries, honey smoked barbecue and roasted jalapenos. These quick snacks may provide energy, but can't substitute for the pleasures of the table.

Even the business world is showing signs of the infestation of the "no time" virus, doing things simultaneously. A *New York Times* article on January 22, 2015, "The One Latte Power Chat," posed this timely question: "Who has time for a two-hour lunch when Twitter is updating?"

In his best-selling book *The Italians,* politician and journalist Luigi Barzini wrote, "Italians eat everything fresh and in its proper season when it is at its absolute best. No fruit or vegetable comes from the hot house with the damp paper taste of artificial products. Nothing is picked before its time and allowed to ripen in storage. Nothing is frozen. Nothing is chemically preserved and everything has the stamp of 'natural.'"

He goes on to describe Italy as having one of the greatest cuisines partly based on the simplicity of its ingredients. "The spirit of Italian cuisine, hospitality open wide to us all, is that of peasant cooking, home cooking, amateur cooking (amateur from *amare*) as cooking with love," he wrote. Barzini may have been right when he wrote that book in 1964. Unfortunately, since that time, globalization has impacted Italy's gastronomic culture as well. The rules of tradition and a culture based on the family table have allowed change to occur at a slower pace than in other industrial countries, but the barriers they have created are weakening. Italy is on the way to losing her food culture.

Having returned to Italy in 2017 after an absence of a few months, I was dismayed to see drastic changes. The market that I frequent once offered six rows of fresh produce. Now it has only four, thanks to two rows now devoted to prepackaged produce. There was a new deli case, too, with prepackaged fish and meat.

Banks in Italy once closed for lunch at one o'clock and opened again for only an hour in the afternoon. Lately I have been surprised to see new hours posted, with banks being open from early in the morning, closed for a two-hour lunch, and then open until six in the evening.

Another disappointment when I returned to Tuscany was noticing road signs directing traffic to a McDonald's. The signs started miles away. Known for being successful in heavy tourist areas in Italy, this new McDonald's location opened its doors near a large Italian commercial center catering more to Italians than tourists. It is the very first in the Validinevole region. I have never seen any other eating establishment with the number of street signs indicating meters and miles. McCafé has been established to attract Italians to the big "M" because they are known to prefer café style snacks over take out.

Hearing that Starbucks, after operating for over thirty-five years around the globe with more than 300 stores in 77 different countries, would establish their first location in Milano, Italy, on Sept. 6, 2018, I must say I was very disappointed, thinking that Starbucks would destroy the coffee bar culture of Italy, a unique aspect of its food culture.

Howard Schultz, Chairman Emeritus of Starbucks gives credit to the Italian coffee culture which he experienced in Milan in the 1980s for inspiring him to develop the Starbucks concept. He was impressed, he says, with the spirit of the Italian people, their love of community, and the excellence of their national drink, coffee. He saw the local bar as a meeting place for neighbors to gather. After that visit in Milan he was inspired to establish and to spread this Italian concept around the world. Spending years researching the Italian culture and society, he waited for the right moment with a concept that could be attractive to Italians as well as by teaming up with Anthonio Percassi, a most successful Italian entrepreneur as his licensee partner. Then to compete with Italian coffee quality which he ascertained he had to do, added the Reserve Roaster that demonstrates the roasting, brewing and mixing of the bean to be enjoyed by customers at the epicenter of fashion and culture in Piazza Cordusio in Milano.

On opening week, seeing the lines to enter the magnificent, 25,000-square-foot spectacular establishment leads me to believe that Starbucks will be successful, but hopefully not eliminate the community hub of every neighborhood in Italy, the coffee bar. It is where the Italian barista's personality and skill in making the national drink are usually the attraction of each neighborhood bar, the center of social life, and an essential part of everyday life for all ages. Open long hours, the coffee bar caters to the local's social, emotional and psychological needs, providing company and conversation to all and especially to any lonesome soul.

Italians tend to enjoy the atmosphere of small intimate bars; meeting and talking to others is often the purpose of going in to get an espresso, more than the need for the actual drink. Gulping down that espresso may involve a quick bar stop or lingering on while standing and talking to whoever is at the bar. Italians do not yet walk down the street with a plastic or paper cup in hand. Italian bars are not for wifi or computer work. Italians like to talk, to hear the neighborhood gossip, to see their friends and to meet new neighbors. This leads me to believe that the 150,000 Italian neighborhood bars may continue to operate. But being that Starbucks' major plan is to establish soon 300 other locations in Italy, I fear that in time, its attraction particularly for youth, may rob Italy of its intimate bar culture, a culture where your favorite barista makes that one order just for you and recognizes you by name, not by an order number.

As an Italian-American, I was so proud that Italy was one of the countries least affected by fast-food establishments. However, if Italy fails to maintain the family bonding, culture, tradition, and life at the table, I fear it will join other countries without food culture, by trading one of the greatest daily pleasures for an epidemic of food disorders, obesity and diet-related illnesses. It is sad that a country known for the quality foods, the dinner hour, the family table, tradition, and culture that made it unique in the world and was envied by many may soon see its demise.

In spite of the changes I observed upon my return to Italy, I did see a ray of hope that food culture may live on. For those who experience food culture in their youth, it is difficult to live without it as an adult, even if going for a walk in outer space. Space food for astronauts came a long way from the Russian's pureed meat squeezed out of a toothpaste-type food tube to the U.S. Mercury mission's bite-size cubes of food and freeze-dried powder accompanied by tubes of semi-liquids. When the Gemini astronauts sneaked a corn beef sandwich into their spaceship to the dismay of NASA, they were disciplined for the floating breadcrumbs that could have caused a detrimental situation. Following this incident, astronauts had to promise to never deviate from the controlled, studied, and allowed foods. Besides the fact that foods have to be nutritious, meet a balanced diet, and be easy to digest and palatable, space foods also have to be light in weight and easy to store, prepare, and consume without any floating particles in zero gravity.

This made favorite foods and special items unacceptable to be brought into the space station. That is until the first Italian spacewalk astronaut, Luca Parmitano, born in Sicily and raised with food culture, prepared for being the first to wear the Italian flag in the vacuum of space. Not wanting to miss a healthy and enjoyable meal along with his crew companions on their five and a half months in outer space, he requested that Argotec, a hundred percent Italian company founded by Dr. David Avino, prepare foods for space that would taste like foods at home, miles away. Argotec is a company of young engineers who research and prepare foods in their space food laboratory to meet the needs of the European Space Agency, as well as foods that give a feeling of home. They work along with the Agenzia Spaziale Italiana, ASI, which sponsored the Volare mission with NASA to prepare Luca's favorite foods according to the recognized knowledge and regulations of NASA. The Italian company was pleased to meet his needs and worked diligently to fulfill his request with specially prepared space foods that would meet the needs of zero gravity, such as veal *scaloppine*, lasagna, *caponata*, and risotto along with Luca's request for tiramisu, his favorite dessert.

The Italian test pilot and astronaut gave his explanation for his request, saying, "Being Italian, I have a special relationship with the culinary arts." In addition to all the usual preparations and the projects that must be accomplished by the astronauts, Luca added a new one. In preparation for his historical Italian spacewalk, he wished "to share a taste of Italian food culture with his colleagues" with genuine foods. The engineers at Argotec accepted the challenge. They succeeded in providing Luca with nutritious, delicious and acceptable foods that Luca could share with his Russian and American crew on his mission. The food, for the first time in space, was one hundred percent organic and salt-free. His actions created the first outer space menu for astronauts. Benvenuto a Il Nido (Welcome to the Nest) was a menu that included the traditional four-course Italian meal to be enjoyed with his crew.

They enjoyed *antipasto of carallucci alla cipolla con crema di pomodori secchi* (carallucci with onions in a cream sauce of sundried tomatoes), *a primo* (first course) of *le lasagne alla Bolognese* (lasagna with meat sauce, Bolognese style) and *il risotto al pesto alla Genovese* (rice with pesto Genovese style), *a secondo* (second course) of *la parmigiana di melanzane* (eggplant layered with parmigiano and other cheeses), and a *dessert* (dessert) of *il tiramisu classico* (rich egg, cream, cheese and coffee dessert).

Luca explained that the Italian chefs and engineers succeeded in providing a delicious Italian meal, balanced with all the necessary dietary needs, and served in microgravity. When asked on returning to earth if there was anything he missed during the Volare mission, Luca commented that the only thing he missed was Italian espresso. Antonio Pillello, the spokesperson for Argotec explained Luca's statement to the public when he said, "You must know that coffee is very important to the Italian people." I may add that it is their national drink.

The Argotec team next had to meet the challenge of fulfilling the requests of the first Italian female astronaut, who flew to the International Space Station in November 2014. When asked by the space food lab what she wanted on her flight, Samantha Christoforetti, a lieutenant and female fighter pilot, requested a nutritious meal and selected possible ingredients. But most important to her was a good cup of Italian coffee. The espresso was a great challenge for Argotec, but having met the requests of Luca, they set out to meet Samantha's needs.

Argotec engineers joined forces with Italian coffee giant, Lavazza, both from Torino, Italy, and ASI, the Italian Space Agency. After a year of studying ways to overcome the limitations imposed by weightlessness, they succeeded in making the first capsule-based espresso coffee system to function in outer space. Samantha became the first in history to sample authentic Italian espresso brewed in outer space while in orbit. Besides holding the longest female record in outer space, 199 days (even longer than any Russian cosmonaut), she also was the first to test the experimental ISSpresso machine 250 miles above the earth as the world's first orbiting barista. She sent back to earth a selfie showing her using the capsules of espresso coffee and sipping from a special cup designed for use in zero gravity. It was a difficult challenge to meet because the coffee machine had to be adapted to the ambient pressure and still not have the color, fragrance and flavor of the coffee altered. The Argotec team realized that when it comes to food and drinks Italians are hard to please, so this was quite an accomplishment.

Luca had commented on his food culture stating that, "One of my projects was to share Italian culture of food with my colleagues." In May 2016, Samantha said how proud she was to be the first barista in outer space. It is her hope that "for the station crew, the coffee may be a venue to get together, chat and relax." You can see how genuine food and *convivio* may have its beginning in outer space thanks to two Italian astronauts who enjoyed it on earth.

Not only has Italy succeeded in being the most popular cuisine in the world with food culture, but thanks to Luca's and Samantha's requests and the Italian space food laboratory Argotec accepting the challenge, along with the cooperation of Agency Spaziale Italiana, the Italians have succeeded in being the first to bring their food culture to outer space. If 2020 sees the gradual decline of Italian tradition and culture on earth, the gastronomic wonders of Italy that steal the spotlight on earth may be about to steal it in outer space.

I believe that in spite of some unfavorable changes occurring in Italy, it will continue to lead the world in food culture and *convivio* because even with limited time most Italians continue to practice the life-enhancing Italian art of eating. I wish in America one could do as most Italians do, rush through work to go to lunch, or shall I say now, dinner? But it will be very difficult for America to change as it has never had food culture, doesn't realize what it is missing, and can't understand its importance. Healthy individual diets are great if they work and should be encouraged, but since behavior is hard to change, Americans must begin with our newborns and expose them to real foods as well as to teach them a sustainable dietary pattern to follow throughout their life. This can occur only if food becomes a priority as it is in Italy. Here granddaughter Kara is munching on kale at five months old and at three years old helping her father make breakfast for her two- and one-year-old brothers.

Food Culture Begins at Home and Succeeds With a Mentor in the Kitchen

During the last thirty years, living in Italy has opened my eyes to what is possible. I have friends who are working mothers, yet they still manage to make a daily family meal. They take some shortcuts, but always make time to cook. Preparing a simple family meal often requires less time than purchasing takeout. There are always exceptions, but my friends were all raised in families where they had their mother or grandmother as mentors in the kitchen. These friends never consider cooking to be drudgery. They see it as challenging and satisfying work that their families appreciate.

My friend Gabbie is a good example. An executive at a design studio, she is happy to take the responsibility of providing nutritious meals for her family in exchange for their sense of well-being. Just as for my mom, for Gabbie it's of the utmost importance to know that her family is eating nutritiously and has time together around the table.

Living with Gabbie for a week, I noticed that she prepared a healthy meal every day in less than thirty minutes. Walking home from work one evening, we stopped by the fish market, where she selected some freshly-cut fillets. At home, she put the slices of merluzza in a frying pan with a little bit of butter and sage. By the time she had prepared a salad dressed with vinaigrette, the fish was done. Our meal was ready in fifteen minutes.

Another day, she put on a pot of water and added chopped garlic, hot peppers, fresh greens, broccoli rabe, and Swiss chard to a skillet while the pasta water came to a boil. While waiting the eight minutes for the pasta to cook al dente, we had time to enjoy a glass of Chianti. The cooked pasta was strained, dumped into the big frying pan of healthy, fresh greens, tossed, and served with some country bread and olive oil. She had made a delicious dinner for five in about twenty minutes.

One morning, I awoke to the wonderful aroma of ribs being sautéed. As we enjoyed our morning coffee, the ribs the butcher had cut for her the day before simmered quietly on the stove. After work that day, she bought a head of red cabbage and added it to the pan with a few spices. It simmered and softened in the delicious juice of the morning ribs and was soon ready to serve.

With just a little planning and prioritizing, Gabbie was able to start her meal in the morning, shop for fresh produce after work, finish cooking when she got home, and serve her family a hot meal in about thirty minutes.

The positive virtue of eating together at a table has been in practice for centuries, from Etruscan and Roman times to the twenty-first century. An individuals' emotional, physical, and psychological well-being can often be correlated to their time at the dinner table.

The Italian dining experience is worth noting, studying, and adopting. In many ways, it has the potential to alleviate or diminish many of the ills of modern society. It is this daily ritual, its significance often overlooked, that plays an important role in the civilization of a country, its values, family life, mores, mannerisms, and social standing. Unfortunately, today's accelerated lifestyle has begun to change life at the family table, even in Italy.

The positive virtues of the Italian dining experience, as well as the negative results observed as Italians gradually move away from the table, leads me to believe that it is time to get back to the table. It can be difficult to find time with the demands of family, work, social obligations, and society, but making time for family meals at the table, without tension or distractions, can be beneficial to all members of the family.

Experiencing the obsession my Italian friends have for genuine foods and life at the table was what led me to look into when food culture actually begins. The Italian parent, obsessed with genuine foods and the health of their children, controls their diet from infancy, seeking a variety of the best seasonal items. Both their Mediterranean diet and their food culture start at an early age. Italian baby food companies have added quality olive oil to their products.

Why is this so important? Because, during the first five years of life, most children accept whatever their parents give them to eat. Italian parents, like most people in countries other than the U.S., encourage their young children to taste a little of everything served at the table, encouraging them to become "neophiliacs," lovers of the new and unfamiliar. By experiencing a variety of ingredients and combinations of flavors, food neophiliacs learn how to accept and, later, to seek out new flavors.

Many of my American friends, on the other hand, are "neophobes." Since they haven't been exposed to variety at the dinner table, they fear new foods and are often set in their ways as to what they will and will not eat. One great example of this is tripe. Most of our foreign friends love tripe, the lining of the cow's stomach, because it is chewy, while many Americans find its chewy texture unfamiliar and unappetizing. The only difference is that most likely Americans haven't had tripe as a child, so they have no experience of eating it stored in their memories. It is up to parents to help their children develop taste buds and educate the palate by giving them new experiences. This will reward them with food culture.

My curiosity as to how food culture begins in a nation like Italy led me to a visit a local nursery school in a farm community in Tuscany. I was able to witness a two-year-old child's first culinary experience away from home. The teacher handed me the menu of the month. This is given to parents in advance, so that they know what their child will eat to avoid duplicating food items at dinnertime. Italians believe that eating seasonally and providing a variety is not only healthier, but also more interesting. Children learn to look forward to mealtime, where they are exposed to a variety of dishes.

Menù invernale Comune di Monsummano Terme

INFANZIA PRIMARIA	PRIMA SETTIMANA INVERNALE	SECONDA SETTIMANA INVERNALE	TERZA SETTIMANA INVERNALE	QUARTA SETTIMANA INVERNALE
LUNEDI	PASTA AL POMODORO BASTONCINI DI PESCE AL FORNO CAROTE FILATE CRUDE FRUTTA FRESCA DI STAGIONE	PENNETTE ALL'OLIO E FORMAGGIO PROSCIUTTO COTTO FAGIOLINI ALL'OLIO FRUTTA FRESCA DI STAGIONE	PASSATO DI VERDURA CON PASTA FRITTATA AL FORMAGGIO CAROTE SALTATE YOGURT ALLA FRUTTA	RISOTTO ALLA PARMIGIANA STRACCHINO PISELLI SALTATI FRUTTA FRESCA DI STAGIONE
MARTEDI	RAVIOLI AL POMODORO MOZZARELLA INSALATA MISTA FRUTTA FRESCA DI STAGIONE	PASSATO DI VERDURA CON RISO COTOLETTA DI POLLO AL FORNO BIETOLA ALL'OLIO FRUTTA FRESCA DI STAGIONE	PASTA AL POMODORO FESA DI TACCHINO AL FORNO PUREA DI PATATE FRUTTA FRESCA DI STAGIONE	PENNETTE ALL'OLIO COSCIA DI POLLO ARROSTO CAROTE LESSE FRUTTA FRESCA DI STAGIONE
MERCOLEDI	PASTA AL PESTO ARISTA AL FORNO PISELLI SALTATI FRUTTA FRESCA DI STAGIONE	PASTA AL RAGU FRITTATA CON PATATE CAROTE FILATE E MAIS FRUTTA FRESCA DI STAGIONE	CREMA DI PATATE E CAROTE CON PANE COTOLETTA DI MARE CAROTE E FINOCCHI FILATI FRUTTA FRESCA DI STAGIONE	PASSATO DI FAGIOLI CON PASTA FRITTATA AL FORMAGGIO INSALATA VERDE DOLCE
GIOVEDI	PASSATO DI VERDURA CON PASTA FRITTATA AL FORMAGGIO PATATE LESSE YOGURT ALLA FRUTTA	RISOTTO AGLI SPINACI IN BIANCO ARISTA AL FORNO INSALATA MISTA FRUTTA FRESCA DI STAGIONE	RISO ALL'OLIO E FORMAGGIO PROSCIUTTO COTTO SPINACI FRUTTA FRESCA DI STAGIONE	PASTA AL POMODORO HAMBURGHER MANZO FAGIOLINI ALL'OLIO FRUTTA FRESCA DI STAGIONE
VENERDI	RISO OLIO E FORMAGGIO POLPETTE DI MANZO IN BIANCO SPINACI ALL'OLIO FRUTTA FRESCA DI STAGIONE	PASTA AL POMODORO STRACCHINO PATATE ARROSTO DOLCE	LASAGNE AL RAGU' BOCCONCINI DI PARMIGIANO INSALATA MISTA FRUTTA FRESCA DI STAGIONE	PASSATO DI VERDURA CON PASTA MERLUZZO AL POMODORO PATATE LESSE FRUTTA FRESCA DI STAGIONE

The school's menu of the month showed the three courses offered daily. The first course, or primo as it is called in Italy, was usually a daily pasta, rice, or soup prepared by the in-house kitchen staff using only healthy ingredients. There were no heavy caloric sauces smothering the freshness of the product. The second course, or secondo, was either fresh fish or meat accompanied by seasonal vegetables. This varied from day to day, introducing these young students to new dishes and tastes. The third course, concluding the meal, was a seasonal fresh fruit, yogurt, or an occasional fruit tart. Eating between meals or away from the table was not allowed. Being satisfied nutritiously reduced the desire for snacking and children were more apt to eat what was being served.

When it was time to eat, the children sat at tables of six. They were served at their tables, thus learning at an early age the importance of eating while seated and appreciating the joy of dining in the company of others. They clearly enjoyed their own style of conversation as well.

All of the children were served the same three-course meals prepared by the school cook. The school nutritionist ensured that all meals met the children's nutritional needs. Children exposed to quality at an early age are likely to continue to make better food choices later in life.

The children were seated a total of thirty minutes, allowing them to use all of their senses to savor each dish and share their excitement for each specialty served. Getting into the habit of allowing plenty of time to eat and enjoy meals carries over into adulthood. It helps cultivate a relaxed attitude toward food, which I have observed in my family and among my Italian friends. I also noted that very little food, if any, was going into the trash.

Visiting my granddaughter Laila's high school in Italy, the International School of Florence, I was not surprised to see three courses offered for the school lunch program. Even the children who brought their lunches from home had their meals carefully packed in three courses.

The SIAF (Servizi Integrati Area Fiorentina) provides lunch with the mission of creating nutritious food with the highest quality ingredients. According to the kitchen's director, the food is sometimes delivered partially prepared, then finished in the on-site kitchen.

The day I visited, the director showed me the seafood salad containing a variety of fresh seafood to which she added fresh quality olive oil, lemon juice, and fresh herbs before serving. She explained that the kitchen gave leftovers to the staff, because each day's menu consisted of fresh ingredients. I was lucky enough to go home with a tray of seafood that supplied my husband and me with our daily requirement of vitamins and minerals, including omega 3, for two days.

In addition to promoting good nutrition, the SIAF emphasizes the importance of taste and table manners and offers educational nutrition programs to support parents and teachers as well as organized field trips to local farms. Like most schools in Italy, over eighty percent of their ingredients are organic.

All it takes is a trip to almost any public school to see how lacking the food culture is in the United States when compared to Italy. I lived in one of the richest communities in Southern California, and when I was invited to a luncheon at a private elementary school, I was shocked to see that the food was delivered by a fast-food provider. Apparently this occurred often and was fully supported by the parents. Since this was a community of highly educated parents, especially compared to the simple farmers in Italy, it surprised me that they accepted this arrangement since the media has clearly reported the potential health concerns and risks associated with the consumption of fast food.

After visiting elementary schools in California and New York, I was also surprised to see that, in most schools, recess plays a more important role than lunch. With only half an hour to both have lunch and play, it's no wonder kids rush through lunch, just as their American parents probably rush through lunch to get back to work.

Many schools have reported huge amounts of wasted food ending up in the cafeteria garbage bins. Why not schedule recess before lunch? Maybe children would eat more slowly, consume more of their food, be more satisfied nutritionally, and not be tempted to want to snack later if they weren't rushing through the meal.

Some American schools are working to improve food quality by providing a selection of fresh vegetables and fruits at lunch and for snacks. Unfortunately, I observed very few students lining up for these healthier options. The school's intentions were good, but the children were still apt to choose the more familiar, low quality foods. I recently heard of an elementary school in Queens, New York that has been successful at serving only healthy and vegetarian meals. They offer no other choices and the children are young enough to learn to eat what is served. Their taste buds are being trained to appreciate, remember, and enjoy real food.

I was pleased when I visited one American elementary school, Anneliese School in Laguna Beach, California, where my grandsons Luca and Dante were attending, that values lunchtime. Six-year-olds were sitting at a table, enjoying the meal prepared by the school's cook, as directed by the school's nutritionist. The teachers supervising the table of youngsters reinforced table etiquette and behavior as I had seen in Tuscany. There were no out-sourced foods, no pre-packaged meals, no fast-food deliveries, and no children running around. The children ate their food at the table and did not throw lunches in the trash. When praising the director, Anneliese, at an event in 2018, she informed me that government officials suggested when she opened her first location that she meet dietary needs with meals from fast-food establishments, as being a practical and time-saving strategy. She refused to do so, and today her schools provide healthy hot lunches, nutritionally balanced and seasonal. She believes if children eat well at the table they will have no need for snacks; how wonderful it would be if more schools could follow the actions of this amazing woman raised in post-war Bavaria, Germany.

To quote a man I most admire and had the pleasure of meeting, President Ronald Reagan, education begins in the home, "for all change in America begins at the dinner table."

Summary of the Four Ingredients of the Italian Diaitan Leading to a Healthier Lifestyle for the Individual, Family and Nation

Living and working in Italy and America, two countries I love, has led me to compare the important role of food culture. America, the most health conscious and industrial country in the Western world, unfortunately leads the industrial world with the most diet-related disorders and diseases. Italy, on the other hand, with these basic ingredients in her food culture, has a less desirable economy but enjoys fewer food-related illnesses and diseases as well as enjoying more longevity than any other country in Europe.

My observations led me to suggest that Americans adopt the four ingredients of the Italian diet for a healthier lifestyle and also that Italy stop the decline of their food culture that I have observed in the last few years, which will lead her to the food epidemic of the 21st century experienced by other countries.

1. Food culture should be introduced at an early age. It is important for parents to introduce children to quality foods before the age of five, when parents are most influential. After five, their environment, the food industry, social media, and the world of marketing become more influential. This is the only way children will have the ammunition to fight the food conglomerates and marketers that have had such a negative influence on making food in America a national dilemma and to keep

Five-year-old enjoying digging out the baby snails to eat before learning social taboos

them from creating becoming a global calamity. I have observed that people who have experienced real food as a child are less apt to be attracted to the industrial product called food.

Rich and poor tend to eat a similar healthy diet in Italy, unlike in America where there is a greater distinction in diet between socio-economic classes. Raised in an Italian household, the only canned items I recall from my childhood were sardines and anchovies, which played an active role, especially on meatless Fridays due to religious restrictions. Mom made amazing dishes with economical small fish, especially considering the wealth of nutrition they have to offer—much more than the

Granddaughter Kara enjoying kale on her own.

large fish popular in most American restaurants. After school or for a snack, a can of these small oil-rich silvery fish always came in handy. I adopted this habit when raising our children before they knew they were eating, head to tail, fish from the sea.

Granddaughter Laila enjoys shrimp, shell and all

When she was only six months old, I introduced sardines (right after bananas) into Michelle's diet. We were on a budget, and I had experienced this in my childhood, so I introduced this delicacy to her. I observed when visiting her years later as an adult that she still loves sardines and eats them as a snack. When she was raising her first child a call came to me asking me how I got her to enjoy sardines, since she was not successful with her daughter Laila. I questioned whether she was giving Laila options. When she answered yes, I told her that was the problem. Children can be taught to eat most items if they are introduced to them at an early age, especially if they are eating the food

Grandson Bo loves black squid ink pasta

with others who enjoy it and have no other options when hungry.

A can of sardines in our household came in handy when there was nothing for dinner. For less than a dollar the two or four sardines in the can could provide daily nutrients for one or two

Grandson Dante's favorite is clams on the half shell

people. Mother would add a little tomato sauce, fresh basil and good olive oil and serve the sardines with some garlic bread and a salad to make a healthy light dinner. A variation might be some lemon and good olive oil dressing on the sardines topped with sliced boiled eggs over a bed of arugula. Or sardines could be added to any salad, such as green beans, with a good olive oil and vinegar dressing. No recipe needed, just a little creativity to produce an inexpensive dinner such as is enjoyed by both the rich and the poor in Italy. No need to go out for fast food. My husband, when living alone in an apartment during his medical residency before we met, said he would add sardines to fried

Grandsons Dante and Luca eating smelts, from head to tail

eggs or put them over a bed of rice for dinner, adding, of course, some good olive oil dressing.

Often when visiting my sister Rose, as I did this February 2018, we both were salivating for a snack when noticed a can of sardines on her shelf. As we dug into our Portuguese sardines in olive oil an American friend came unannounced. Seeing what we were enjoying, with a disgusted look on her face she inquired as to what in the world were we eating.

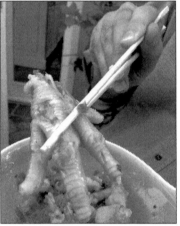

Son Jason enjoying chicken feet as an adult, just as he did as a five-year-old

As for anchovies, I often introduce them as my secret ingredient hidden in dishes that I serve to our guests who claim to hate anchovies. Happy to say, we have served and changed the opinions of many non-anchovy eaters after they experienced them at Villa Lucia in various dishes or enriching many favorite sauces. Nevertheless,

they may never appreciate them with such memories as do those who have had the experience of enjoying them in childhood.

Neophiles enjoy so many delicacies offering many new culinary experiences, such as less expensive cuts of meats or tiny fish that are not popular but are rich in nutrients. If a child is not exposed at a young age they will often remain a neophobe, eating only recognized foods. Even if they do occasionally try new items as an adult to gain social mobility, since they lack the memories the food from youth, this will have little impact on changing behavior.

2. The public should demand to know what they are consuming, how it was prepared, and from where the item has journeyed. This would lead the industry to be more honest about their ingredients and preparation. Packaged and prepared food labels must not deceive the public, who could make better choices if products were properly labeled. Children would be less attracted to "Carcass and Bone Nuggets"—a more accurate name for an industrial product often referred to as chicken nuggets. Similarly, "Chemical Fries" is a more appropriate name for fast food French fries when potato is only one of 18 ingredients, and "Industrial Frozen Desert" is the name I would give items with 15 unfamiliar ingredients trying to pass as artisan ice cream.

A nation without food culture will tend to have little interest in the history of an item, in comparison to food culture nations. They will settle for that which the industry markets best for profit unless they become cognizant of what they are eating and become more demanding for real food.

Seeing the boiled eggs sold in grocery stores confirms the lack of interest in the kitchen among Americans, despite the number of food-related TV shows in the U.S. These pre-boiled eggs give one no history of the product. Where did it come from? When was the hen hatched? How was it fed? Where? Country? Farm? How old? Open air? Biological? Caged? Does anyone care? In Italy, a food culture country, the customer wants to know and the government requires that every egg sold has its history stamped on it. When there is a health issue one need not destroy all the eggs in the country; instead, we can go to the source. This is a sample of the history of eggs purchased in Italy where all of the above is noted on each egg.

Americans buying prosciutto may not be interested in knowing the history of the animal. But in Italy the customer wants to know. If a product proves to be defective, one can go to the source. A piglet's leg is tattooed with its history. One

knows where it was raised, fed, housed and slaughtered. Americans do not seem to have an interest in this. At one establishment our class saw how the outer fat of the pig's leg was cut to show the customer how the establishment

can verify the final product. The establishment noted that they did not feed the animal, as could be learned

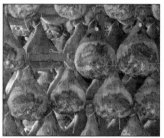

by looking at the pyramid shaped cutting in the outer fat. To the left are pigs fed by others, to the right those fed by the establishment we visited. An informed customer makes healthier choices.

Often in Italy I have been served at hotel breakfast buffets honey right from the honey comb. Discussing how pleased I was to see this, our waiter on one

occasion explained that Italians like to see the comb to verify that it is real honey. Up until then ignorant of synthetic honey, I was informed how many honeys on the market never saw a bee or the bee never saw a flower. This surprised me, but in my research proved to be true.

Globalization has brought new challenges. Products moving between countries encounter different laws and regulations. This also makes it more difficult to trace the history of a product, especially when dealing with a public that has no interest in or concern about what they are consuming. Deception is more universal in the case of countries without food culture. A perfect example of the difficulty of determining the source of the foods we eat was described in a February 2013 issue of the Week Magazine in an article titled "The Journey of the Hamburger." It explained how horse meat was being sold as ground beef. Horse meat has been sold for consumption for centuries in many countries as good quality meat, but like all foods it should be labeled properly and pass inspection by health and government authorities before being offered to the public, which unfortunately is not always the case.

In this situation the meat came from a Romanian *abattoir* (slaughterhouse). A farmer sold horses that were not bred for human consumption to an agent in the Netherlands. This was the first unregulated step in a long chain of uncontrolled transactions through some ten counties before the meat reached the dinner table of an unsuspecting family. The Netherland agent sold it to an agent in Cyprus who supplied meat to a factory in Luxembourg that sold it to a French company that supplied meat to a Swedish company that made frozen dishes branded by a British company. The British company sold their products to France, Germany, Sweden, Norway, Holland and Poland as hamburger meat. When illness appeared, it took a great deal of time and effort to determine what the cause was. The investigation eventually led to a "beef" lasagna that traced back to the slaughterhouse in Romania. In addition to the fact that the meat did not come from a regulated horse bred for human consumption, the toxic substance phenylbutazone was found in the meat. The individuals responsible for these deceptions were arrested, but the question remains. Was it an accident, or was the profit motive the reason that the meat was allowed to pass uncontrolled through the doors of ten countries?

3. Children should experience life in the kitchen, the heart of the home, and find pleasure in shared work, which should be creative and not a chore. Allow children to absorb the wisdom of the cuisine by using their senses to listen to the

sizzle of meat on the grill, smell the yeasty smell of rising bread dough, hear the clicking of utensils, inhale the aromas of a homemade chicken broth, and relish the tastes of a plate of comfort food. Parents should instill eating habits that will help sustain life and not stress children over a confusing list of rules and diets that can be more detrimental than the food itself and destroy the joy of eating. Get back into the kitchen with the family, creating an enjoyable and fun experience not to be considered drudgery. Children have a greater appreciation of foods if they know where they come from.

Our grandchildren, when they were in grammar school, came to visit us in Tuscany during Easter break as we were planting our tomato plants. They were so excited when they came for the summer to see all the rows of vine-ripe tomatoes waiting to be picked. It was fun for them at first, but after days of picking I decided to give them a break by giving them the opportunity to start canning the tomatoes for the winter. That also was fun, at least for the first 100 bottles. Needing a change in activities, I directed my poor overworked grandchildren to start cleaning the crate of cherry tomatoes they had picked to get them ready for the oven. I can still hear Bo asking his sister Laila, "Why did we pick so many?" Their reward was a great dinner of cherry tomatoes roasted in our wood burning oven (another lesson learned) to top freshly made pasta.

Four generations making empanadas—

Jorge

*Laila and her two
great-grandmothers*

Son Jason with his grandmother and great aunts

Jorge cleaning shrimp for the barbecue with our three kids, then doing the same with our grandchildren Bo and Laila

4. Families should return to the family table and not allow family fun at mealtimes to fall by the wayside, thereby preserving this underrated commodity. The table could be the means to maintaining the stability of the family and be the best vehicle to bring family and friends together to enjoy precious moments, traditions, and togetherness. Eating slowly in a pleasant environment and appreciating one item at a time boosts digestive efficiency and nutrient absorption. How we eat is as important as what we eat. For Italian Americans like myself, eating foods according to the rules of tradition and culture is essential to cultural and family preservation. Eating together at the table elevates the biological process to refuel the body to the rituals of family and community. This creates a more relaxed attitude to food and the eating process, which is healthier than being constantly worried about following rules and diets.

When he was nine years old, our son Jorge had a school assignment to write about his family. I want to share his conclusion to the six-page report graded A-plus, with a picture of our family and comments on our family table.

> I think my family is an interesting one because of our background. I learn different things from my Spanish grandma and Italian grandma. They give us culture, language and habits, from their old country. In our house the dinner table may have three different languages. I am happy they are all so different. We are a close family that shares problems together. My grandparents can help us and teach us when my parents aren't around. We have an old European customs of living together and eating together.

My life around the table will continue in Abruzzo. Here we are with some 24 expats from various countries who have settled in our community and enjoy *convivio* together. As Dante said some 700 years ago, the table is a place to learn knowledge, gain wisdom and enjoy companionship. I am sure if more could find the time for *convivio*, a happier world it could be.

The time saved by not eating good meals at a table could very well cost years of life lost. The money we think we're saving by buying poor quality foods may actually cost us more later, when we have to pay for more medical prescriptions and doctor's visits. Failing to make time at the table can lead to physical, social, economic and psychological problems later in life. Ralph Waldo Emerson was right when he said, "There is no greater wealth than health." The Mediterranean Diaitan, which includes these four noted ingredients, including *convivio*, has proven to lead the individual, the family and the nation to a healthier way of life.

APPENDIX

B & B FIRST NEWSLETTER, 1986 (Things have changed in the last 30 years.)

My B& B Brochure 1986

Our First Year as a B and B

In retrospect, the first year of our bed and breakfast experience in Italy has been a great success. Yes, as our guests arrived, we still had some minor remodeling to do. Trying to remodel a 15th century farmhouse to meet the needs of our 20th century guests has not been an easy task, especially in a foreign land with foreign workers who have strange, or shall I say, different work habits.

✦ Friends and strangers came from France, Spain, England and, of course, the USA. California guests came from Pasadena, San Diego, La Jolla, Fallbrook, San Francisco and Newport Beach. What was supposed to be an intercultural experience for my guests has been a mutually rewarding experience for me and for our Italian neighbors.

✦ The Spaniards, in first gear at midnight, eat at 10:00 and then are ready for action in town. The English, even while exploring the Etruscan ruins, find time to stop for 5:00 tea. The French, amazed by our Puritanism, cannot comprehend the negativism in bathing topless. Then come the Americans, the most interesting to watch in Europe, who learned a great deal about Italian mores and mannerisms:

✦ John – the hard way to use the bidet; Susan – how expensive luggage can be when you need an extra taxi to carry it; Judy – the green lettuce escarole does not crawl; Lois – spiders in the bathroom can be harmless; Kathleen – that Italian men's reputation for boldness can also be charming. Our Phoenix friends will never forget the word scuppero (strike) as they waited for the train that would arrive the next day.

✦ They all learned to: drink coffee standing at the local bars, to sit would cost them double; to eat pannini (sandwiches) without mayonnaise and good Italian bread without butter. Sandra now knows the difference between gas oil and benzina as the station attendant patiently siphoned the gas out of her diesel car engine as the Italians in the gas line observed in awe. Ron, our 21-year old Newport Beach pizza maker, invented a new pizza cooked in our wood-burning oven. Nobody told him to remove the ashes so we had pizza ala Hickory Farm.

✦ I also learned a great deal. Americans are coffee addicts. As Europeans consume their ounce of espresso in the morning with or without milk, the Americans fill their 8 ounce cup with pure dark espresso as if it were orzo and then proceed for their second or third. We are also the world's ice cube consumers, possibly having something to do with our consumption of hard alcoholic beverages.

✦ Some of us shopped at the Pratese's second-hand store, where beautiful, supposedly imperfect embroidered linen sheets can cost up to $2,000. Others enjoyed shopping at Collodi for suitcases filled with Pinocchio dolls to take home to the little ones. Newport Beach women went crazy in Montecatini, ten minutes down the hill, at

Fendi, Versace, Gucci, Gianfranco, Georgio Armani and Ferragamo to note a few. One husband's remark: "Lucy, how could you do this to me? You said we were going to a farm and she spent $5,000 at Fendi's!"

✦ What do the country folk think of Americans? To our farming neighbors, Nicola and his family, who joined Jack from Newport and his party for their final night dinner, the answer was spedicioni (spenders). Thanks go to artist Dick of San Diego, who sent me beautiful spendicioni T-shirts he painted with Montevettolini in the background. To my furniture renovator, after meeting a group from the States, exclaimed, "They don't look like the Carringtons." Obviously, popular US programs throughout Europe are Dallas and Dynasty. To the former police chief of our province, Americans seem to love to go barefoot. He would watch in amazement as Kathleen, our painter from Fallbrook who spent a month with us, would work barefoot in the yard.

✦ But the party that created the greatest interest was our first guests from Pasadena: bride, groom and wedding party. Why would this California girl want to get married in our Romanesque, 12th century church on a farming hilltop in Montevettolini? Maybe she saw A Room with a View. As the wedding party appeared for the marriage ceremony, all the farmers eyed the beautiful American bride in the white mini wedding dress. Our parish priest died shortly before the wedding (like a scene from a Fellini film), so a local priest substituted. God forgive me! He could not take his eyes off Renée's beautiful legs. As Sandra, who made all the wedding arrangements said, "Montevettolini will never be the same now that the Americans have arrived."

✦ Is Fellini really a genius or does Italy constantly create theatrical scenes? There is no doubt that the true Italian is found in the country. Simple, genuine, with uninhibited emotions and little need to hide feelings, he has not yet been influenced by the industrial civilization, which makes robots out of all of us as we conform to convention. As Orson Welles once said: "The Italian has the facility to express emotions. Their only drawback is when they become an actor and must turn to reading and hamming, for then he becomes rigidly controlled." Yes, Mr. Welles, country folks particularly communicate abundantly and efficiently with gestures and movements. (The priest said nothing, but his eyes expressed his true feelings.) Yes, I have learned to admire their natural and instinctive expressions of emotion, which is learned from childhood. This also explains why they are often unhappy in societies where people hide emotions or speak with blank faces.

✦ When I questioned our wonderful neighbors, farmers and local contemporary artisans that I was fortunate to befriend as to why they always seem happy in spite of the inevitable problems that life conceives, their answers were direct and simple. One must work their lifetime so it is important that work be pleasurable. Work should not be a punishment. My ironsmith, who works with a gleam in his eye while listening to Vivaldi said, "My energy comes from pride in my work." My ceramic artisan, who always greets me with a smile and a quote from Dante or Socrates pertaining to his day or his work, said, "Laughter cleans out the lungs and brings fresh oxygen to your system and is addicting to those around you." When I added that it did not solve problems, he added, "Neither does crying."

✦ These insights into the country life in Italy cannot be expressed by reading guide books, which may inform us of the art, history and men of antiquity, but not the contemporary Italian. His experience, expressions, gestures and mannerisms cannot be comprehended by the written word. This may be the last generation of an Italian society not influenced by northern adaptations and self- controlled manners.

✦ In the country, there is still evidence of love, sensuality and security, which are essential ingredients of a life style where the human element prevails. Are they less productive? Maybe so financially, but I would observe that they have mastered an art difficult to master and that is the art of being happy and making others happy, regardless of their social and economic status. Each trip back to California allows me greater objectivity of our society and life. I see greater productivity, more streets, more buildings, more people rushing about, but I also see the faces that seem void of emotion. At times I thought the Italian country and southern people were too emotional, but now I view them as being natural, with genuine expression and feelings and not as inhibited as we are. How can one make others happy without expressing happiness oneself?

✦ When we started remodeling in September of 1985, our first friend came to visit. As our San Clementine surfer watched the sand blasters fill the air with white clouds of old plaster and stones of centuries ago, and the mason drilling holes into our three foot 15th century wall, he looked at the multitude of trucks and workers and said, "Why here? You could have bought on Ortega Highway back home." Well Gordon, it may be hard for some to understand but it is not the farm but the intercultural experience I sought, a complete contrast to the Newport Beach lifestyle. Yes, Milan and Rome could offer me the same things as Los Angeles and New York, as can most northern European cities: People who, in general, act, dress, work and look alike as they hurry about being productive, watching their clock, rushing to make deadlines and popping Maalox in their mouth between gulps of alcohol. As the world shrinks, so does individuality. The big city hotels get to look alike and all have English speaking employees and the omnipresent

✦ To experience the true Italy, as in most countries, one should experience life in the country. In Montevettolini, tradition is still intact. The family unit is visible, as well as the zest for life that goes with a three-hour lunch break and simple, healthy and natural cuisine.

✦ When the Samson party of 15 arrived for a two-week stay to celebrate the elders' 50th wedding anniversary at our farm, it was time for me to leave. There was no room at the inn for the innkeeper. After showing them around both house and town, I left on a 1:30 a.m. train to head north and home. As I left the family of 15 seated around the dining room table, I realized how much I had learned from this first year experience. Their stay was a wonderful conclusion to our first year in business, which began with the wedding party from Pasadena and ending with the 50th wedding anniversary of the couple from Huntington Beach and Los Angeles.

✦ As for special memories, there are too many to note and some never to reveal. But to touch upon a few: our visit to the Grotta Glusti, Europe's most famous grotta five minutes from our farm, where eight of us experienced the health benefits of the mineral waters in the caverns of heaven, purgatory and hell; our special night in Florence at my favorite trattoria where Quinto - owner, chef, waiter and former opera singer – sang to us a rendition of melodies from Tosca; our beautiful day in Portofino, Italy's picturesque cove on the Italian Riviera; our day in Venice, watching the summer gondola race.

✦ To my neighboring farmers, "To be rich means to be yourself and to be happy with yourself: Make the most of what you have and live with honor." On a monetary scale, he might not be rich but when one meets him one knows he believes, acts and is convinced that he has the world in his hands; good friends, family, lots of love and land to survive on. I begged my picture framer to skip his three-hour lunch so that my frames would be done in two days instead of ten. He looked at me and without expressing a word communicated. Being Italian, I understood his gestures and facial expressions. Who am I to command him of his time? He later told me that time is life's gift. Each one should use it as he wishes. What right do I have to ask him to skip his lunch and the daily family gathering to meet the needs of my guests that were to arrive in one week? Sometimes I wish this ideal philosophy could be adopted by our industrial society, which sees it as unrealistic. The artisans all seem to be in control of their life and time – God's gift. How sad that we reach the stage where the use of this gift is determined by others.

✦ Yes, it may be good to go home where life is more organized, all can be seen clearly, words have definite meaning and laws are made to be followed. But as our guests expressed, the relaxing, mild way of life in the country can be addicting, making the return to our fast-paced competitive society and one's organized hourly calendar schedule less desirable. Still today, after living part of last three years in Italy, when the bell of St. Michelle and Montevettolini sound off the hour and the real live coo-coo birds tell me a new day is here, I am rewarded with a spiritual uplift as I open the bedroom shutters. Somehow, back home, the screeching alarm clock and constant ring of the telephone fail to invigorate my adrenaline system with a smile of sincerity that the land of my ancestors invokes. In summary, to me, la Dolce Vita is no longer Via Vento, Fifth Avenue, Rodeo Drive or the Champs Elysée. La Dolce Vita still can be found if one can learn to appreciate, understand and adapt the mores and mannerisms of the Italian country folk. Stop fretting over life's imperfections, envying what others have and do and by finding dignity in one's self and what one does. Most of all, one must learn the basic, refreshing pleasures of simplicity

■ EYE ON DP

All in the Family

Third generation at Luciana's keeps family legacy 30 years strong

By Andrea Papagianis
Dana Point Times

When Lucia put olive oil on the restaurant table, it was innovative. Waiters ran back-and-forth as customers requested butter for their bread, but the first generation Italian-American stayed strong, held her ground and figured people would eventually come around. She was right.

In 1978, Lucia "Lucy" Luhan became one of the first Orange County restaurateurs to offer fresh, handmade pastas. With her mother, Mary Vallera, in the kitchen of their What's Cooking Bistro in Newport Beach, she served pasta, not spaghetti, to her eatery's patrons. Pastas delicately highlighted by sauces, meats, cheeses and vegetables, Lucia held true to her mother's traditional ways to introduce a community to Italian "food culture." And for the last 30 years, things have remained relatively unchanged.

"The Italian recipe is simple, its good ingredients and creativity," Lucia Luhan said.

Lucia expanded her restaurant portfolio with a second location in the What's Cooking line in Costa Mesa. She'd follow it in 1983 with Luciana's Ristorante in Dana Point. Straying slightly from the simple, take out cafe with a deli and small bistro tables, Lucia kept it simple and created an Italian, Mediterranean escape along the Southern California coast.

This month Luciana's celebrates its 30th anniversary, and although Lucia is no longer the face in the day-to-day operations, her name and son, Jorge Luhan II, ensure her vision and the Italian "convivira," literally translated to "living together," tradition of gathering around the table live on.

"Knees under the table," as my father used to say," recalled Lucia of her family's meals at the table.

The Vallera family left their home in the Abruzzo province, east of Rome and the Lazio region in central Italy in the late-1930s, but like many immigrants brought their cultural customs along. Among her favorites, Lucia recalls meals stretching for hours, her mother's art of homemade pastas, garden, cellar and her values that helped bring numerous family members stateside.

Mary began making pasta when she was just 6 years old. It was a skill that became second-nature after decades of mixing, rolling and cutting the creations daily. From the family's first restaurant in their settled Connecticut to Luciana's, Mary was a regular fixture in the kitchens making her pastas. Ignoring her daughter's pleas to use a machine, Mary held firm to the way she was taught, crafting each pasta hand.

"You cannot make it (pasta) as good as you can by

Mary Vallera made handmade pastas daily for her family and Luciana's Ristorante customers well into her 90s. Courtesy photo

For 30 years, the Vallera-Luhan family has shared Italian traditions with south Orange County at Luciana's Ristorante. Now with the reins, Jorge Luhan II (right) is carrying on the legacy of the woman before him, his mother, Lucia Luhan (left) and grandmother, Mary Vallera. Photo by Rick Davitt

hand," Lucia said. "There is a warmth of the hand that makes the dough better, and anyway, she makes it faster by hand than by machine."

Well into her 90s Mary continued her artisanal craft, that for over 27 years, patrons throughout the family's Orange County restaurants feasted upon. For more than a decade after Jorge and his brother Jason took over the operations, Mary was unrelenting. But as her dexterity dwindled and it became increasingly more difficult to navigate a bustling restaurant kitchen, Jorge "fired" his grandmother, he quipped.

"We have kind of retired her for now. If we needed her to help she could, but it'll be just a little bit slower than before," Lucia said of her mother's pasta making, who just a few years ago shared her craftsmanship with adoring visitors of her daughter's Italian countryside cooking school.

In 1985, Lucia took the family operation international. Long waiting to return to the homeland her parents left behind, the Connecticut born and raised Lucia jumped on an opportunity and purchased a forgotten 500-year-old Tuscan farmhouse. Sitting upon 18-acres of olive groves, Lucia began picking and pressing her own olive oil that same year. Luciana's has been serving the Villa Luciana oil ever since.

Each October, Lucia takes to the groves and handpicks olives from the trees for pressing. It's a knowing where food comes from and how it is made that goes back to mankind's beginning. The concept, Jorge believes, his mother and grandmother were ahead of the times in bringing fresh produce, handmade items and the Mediterranean diet to the Orange County table, when society had strayed.

"You look at trends and you get to watch them come full circle," Jorge said.

The Luhans now have plans to market their line of oils. With European Union credentials obtained, they hope to have the U.S. Food and Drug Administration's approval in time for December bottling. Lucia's passion for food and culture is apparent when she talks about olive oil.

From mislabels and rancid products to health benefits and recipes, she has spoken on the olive oil topic for decades. A 2010 study from the UC Davis Olive Center found that 69 percent of extra virgin olive oil imports sold

On Sunday, October 13 Mary Vallera's descendants gathered to celebrate their matriarch's 100th birthday. Photo by Rick Davitt

by California retailers failed to meet a U.S. Department of Agriculture quality standard. And while some are better for frying than drizzled over vegetables, Lucia said the healthy oils are pungent, bitter and slightly sting the back of your throat.

While officials work out the olive oil regulation kinks, Lucia is happy to see her mother's diet, heavy with the medicinal and nutritional "liquid gold"—for stomach aches, moisturizer, popcorn, pasta and scrambled eggs—olive oil has become a prominent part of American society.

"America gave me a lot of things, but it did not give me food," Lucia said. "I was born and raised here, met my husband here and raised my children here. America gave me everything. But thank god my mother gave me food culture."

Mary's time-honored craft is one Lucia fears will soon be a lost art, and her traditions forgotten. The family's matriarch turned 100 this month, and celebrated her birthday surrounded by generations on Sunday, October 13. Deeply rooted in Italian customs, Jorge, who has led the Luciana's operations for 20 years now, said the way of the past is here to stay.

"We have changed slightly with the times, but we will never leave behind who we are or what we are," Jorge said. ■

MOTHER-IN-LAW'S 100th
IN ARGENTINA

Jorge dancing with his mother

When she was 80, we promised my mother-in-law that if she made it to 100 we would fly to Argentina for her birthday. So we had to keep our promise.

In Memoriam

Maria Concetta Vallera

Oct. 9, 1913 – Nov. 26, 2018

My mother, Mary Concetta Vallera, was a shining example of the benefits of the Mediterranean diaitan. She never told us what, how or when to eat, but from an early age she exposed us to her traditions and life in the kitchen. She inspired us with her food culture and passion for food, family, and friends enjoying convivio. Here is mom at her 105th birthday celebration with loved ones, singing along with Donna Mosello at the accordion, on October 9, 2018. She enjoyed life without ever dieting, following food trends, reading diet books, going to the gym or taking vitamins. Food was her medicine and *convivio* was her enjoyment. We lost her a few weeks after this party when she died in her sleep after telling me for the last time, "I love you. Buona notte, Lucia."

Luhans Hoping All Enjoy *Convivio*, December 2018

Lucy Ann and her husband, Dr. Jorge Luhan, with their immediate family: Michelle Luhan Nordberg, husband Peter, and their children, Laila Ann and Robert (Bo) Barren; Jorge ll and his wife, Dr. Anne Luhan, and their children, Kara Anne, Kai Andrew and Kaden Anders; and son Jason and his wife, Jennifer Luhan, and their children, Luca Scott and Dante Eric.

For more information, please visit Lucy's website, www.lucyluhan.com, where you'll find a full-color gallery of all images in *Convivio* as well as related content. Visit Amazon to purchase a full-color Kindle edition.

Made in the USA
Middletown, DE
15 March 2019